Muffin Dog Press Companion Series

Presents

Beginning English Rider's Companion

All About Horses and Riding for Young Riders, Their Parents, and Adult Beginners

There has never been a riding book like this, dedicated to answering the questions that vex parents of young riders, and adults new to the sport. It is intended to bring new 'horsepeople' into the world of English Riding as quickly and thoroughly as possible; it can be part of a comprehensive training program, preferably with the in-person assistance of an able trainer; those with some experience and their own horse might find its hints and exercises useful for enhancing their enjoyment of riding, and improving their riding skills.

Acknowledgements and Dedication

In addition to the teachers and trainers cited at the end of this book, I would like to thank a number of horses, especially:

Blaze, for helping me learn to canter and jump.

Maple, the most miserable large pony you'd ever want to meet, who helped me learn to discipline a horse immediately if not sooner, exceeded only by...

Scarlet, another large pony, who reinforced the lesson.

Madam, a perfect horse, who taught me to wait to the jumps.

Kindlewood, a kind, talented Thoroughbred I leased from Lisa Brown Baker of Journey's End Farm; the late K. Woodley Esq. (as I affectionately called him) was my best friend, until I bought...

Major Yeats, my beloved horse for the past 18 years, now semi-retired and enjoying a life of occasional trail rides a mile from where he was born in the beautiful Appalachian foothills of Southwest Virginia/Northeast Tennessee. Yeats kept his promise to me, and I kept mine to him. He never ran up vet bills I could ill afford, and I retired him when he was young enough to enjoy being a horse.

This book is dedicated to my Hunter-Jumper, Major Yeats, who—one way or another—taught me everything I know.

And to Peter Krukoski of Fox Hollow Riding Academy in Bristol, TN, the trainer who found Yeats for me, sold Yeats to me, and helped me with Yeats' early training, and has remained a friend ever since.

Muffin Dog Press

Beginning English Rider's Companion

All About Horses and Riding for

Young Riders,

Their Parents, and

Adult Beginners

by

Laura Harrison McBride

ISBN-13: 978-0-9816095-0-8
ISBN-10: 0-9816095-0-3

Library of Congress Control Number: 2008903571
Library of Congress subject heading: Horsemanship

Please visit the publisher's website for information about upcoming releases. Visit www.muffindogpress.com.

Please visit the author's personal website at www.LauraHarrisonMcBride.net.

Muffin Dog Press
P.O. Box 413
New Windsor, MD 21776

DISCLAIMER

No book can teach a person to ride horses. Riding is an active pursuit, and for safety, it is necessary to take lessons with a qualified professional trainer. While the author of this book is a qualified trainer, the information is based on her experience alone, and therefore is a guide, not a complete exposition of all that is necessary to become a good and safe rider.

NOTE WELL: Because of the inherent danger of working with large animals, and because riding is an active pursuit and may result in injuries as any other sport, it is necessary to seek the in-person assistance of a qualified trainer for safety's sake.

Neither the author nor publisher is responsible for any mishap or injury that may occur as a result of the reading or application of information in this book, whether or not it is used in concert with the assistance of a qualified trainer.

However, it is strongly advised that you seek the assistance of a qualified trainer before attempting to ride a horse of any sort, for any reason.

Beginning English Rider's Companion

Table of Contents

Introduction 1
Chapter One: Why We Ride 5
Chapter Two: Is Riding a Dangerous Sport? 17
Chapter Three: Benefits of Riding 23
Chapter Four: Equine Dollars and Sense 29
Chapter Five: Your Kingdom for a Horse? 35
Chapter Six: Finding Lessons 53
Chapter Seven: Basic Equipment for Safe Riding 67
Chapter Eight: Getting Ready to Ride 87
Chapter Nine: Mounting 109
Chapter Ten: Walk and Halt 121
Chapter Eleven: About the Art of Riding 143
Chapter Twelve: A Good Walk and a Trot 151
Chapter Thirteen: More Walking, More Trotting 165
Chapter Fourteen: Cantering 181
Conclusion 185
Appendices: Glossary, equine studies, and useful
catalogs 187
Glossary 189
Colleges Offering Equine Studies 209
Catalogs 215
Books Cited 219
About the Author 221

Introduction

Lots of people think the horsemanship in *Lonesome Dove* is one of the best parts of the movie. In fact, to horse people, it was one of the worst. In *Lonesome Dove*, cowboys jumped onto untrained horses and rode happily into the sunset.

Of course, that was the romantic notion of someone who had obviously never met an untrained horse and tried to ride it, and obviously didn't consult with the author of the book the movie was based on: Larry McMurtry grew up on a Texas ranch, and would have understood how unrealistic it was. But it was Hollywood types that were responsible for translating the material for the screen. Having wild men jump onto wild horses was a sure-fire viewer draw...not unlike train wrecks and shark attacks.

It is true that there might be some extremely tractable horse somewhere that one could jump onto, spurs and all—even if that horse had not had a minute of training. But I would just as soon pin my livelihood to lottery tickets as pin my riding pleasure to that possibility.

Horses are, to all intents and purposes, wild animals. Unlike dogs, they rarely, if ever, regard their owners with unconditional love and loyalty. They are, however, amenable to what we want to do with them.

> **The horse has so docile a nature that he would always rather do right than wrong, if he can only be taught to distinguish one from the other.**
> —Scottish writer George Melville (1821–1878)

Rather, horses obey their riders, if the horses are properly trained and not rogues. And they often enjoy a ride, if the rider is skillful or at least tactful, and lets the horse do at least some naturally horsey things. In fact, that's one of the intrinsic charms of the horse: It is not going to do tricks for you for treats, or just because it likes you, or because you saved it when it had been dumped at the animal shelter. A horse does whatever it does because it is convinced that doing that thing is in its own best interests. That means, of course, that the rider must be able to interact on an equal footing with what some (non-riders) would regard as a lower life form. (Those of us who know horses understand that they are among the noblest of beasts.) It might also be why most riders own dogs as well as horses. The horse is their partner; the dog is their friend.

Despite their wild nature, horses are usually willing to be in a relationship with a human. Stephen Budiansky, in his great book, *The Nature of Horses*, proposed that it was the horse that first sought out man, in order to avail himself of grain in the winter in return for allowing the human to use his 'horsepower' for work. One cannot know that for certain, but it is certain that man would have had a hard time getting close to a horse eons ago, when wild things were much more wild, without the horse's complicity.

Nonetheless, one of the closest relationships any human has in his or her life is the one with a horse, especially a horse bought early and owned long. The give-and-take of riding creates a bond that is strong, unique and most often spiritual. If the rider later becomes the trainer of his or her own horse, the bond becomes stronger still. Most pleasure-horse owners will tell you that, when their horse goes to the great paddock in the sky, they expect to have to be locked up in a rubber room for a while, because of the intensity and depth of their grief. Indeed, all the riders I know who have experienced this trauma describe it as very like losing a beloved friend or family member (as it is with dogs and cats), but worse. In fact, it seems well nigh indescribable.

When he was a young teenager, one English riding instructor in East Tennessee slaved on his father's farm for several summers to earn enough money to buy a horse. He had not had the horse long when it had a positive Coggins, which meant it was carrying Equine Infectious Anemia. And that meant that the horse had to be put down. The boy never recovered from the loss. He never bought another personal horse. When he was a man, he did, however, buy a horse farm and started a riding academy.

For that man, owning a dozen or more school horses was far different from owning his very own horse. He cared for and about his school horses, but they were tools of his trade, not his best friends. His grief over the loss of his first horse was palpable 30 years after the event.

One way or another, a horseperson will always have a horse. The downside to horse ownership—even grief—is more than balanced by the upside. But what is that upside?

A look at Chapter One will tell you **Why We Ride**.

Chapter One: Why We Ride

Why do people ride horses? First, there is the opportunity to create a partnership across species, something that happens, perhaps, only with horse riders, camel drivers and Indian mahouts and their elephants.

Even then, I'm only surmising. I've never met a camel driver nor a mahout. Perhaps K-9 cops experience some of this in their partnership with their dog. But still, it is rare that a human depends so thoroughly on a partner who doesn't speak in human language, is as much as ten times larger than the human, can easily kill a human and is, as noted before, essentially a wild animal. This is a far cry from pairs figure skating, possibly the most well-known partnership sport on the planet.

English riding, under discussion here, includes hunt seat, from which one learns to jump, and it includes dressage, which is the equine equivalent of dancing and involves no jumping. Eventing—cross-country jumping— is also an "English" discipline. This book deals with hunt seat specifically, although getting a grounding in hunt seat makes it easy to learn dressage as well. In my experience, the transition works better in that direction than the other way.

One learns much from interaction with horses. One learns discipline and courage from horses; this is especially true in English riding. One learns persistence. One learns to look at the big picture, and mind the details as well. One learns selflessness and empathy. One learns not to take one's self too seriously. One learns that it is the quality of the journey, not the reaching of the destination, that is important.

Indeed, it is rare that a rider—or a rider's parent— behaves like ice-skating's Tonya Harding and assumes that winning is the only part of the sport worth having. In fact, many people never compete in shows, learning to ride only for the joy of doing it and their own pleasure.

Even in the upper echelons of show jumping, however, doing *anything* to win will get one warned off the sport for good. ♥ If winning at all costs is your philosophy, this book is not for you.

If you want to learn to ride safely, have some fun, and perhaps enjoy showing for the sport of it, then this book can help you reach your goals. Learning to ride is an active pursuit, and is best done on horseback, not in the pages of books, as the section on Discipline, below, will show you. Rather, this book is a touchstone, providing some helpful background, some ways to think about horses and horsemanship, and some exercises you might find useful.

What one learns from horses

Discipline: One of my adult students has asked me a minimum of 1,000 times if I think she has the capability of learning to ride well. Yes, I tell her. She is healthy and has a good mind.

In fact, there are no impediments but one: she refuses to believe and practice the

First Rule of Learning to Ride:

Apply the seat of the pants to the seat of the saddle, as often as reasonably possible.

♥ In 1995, "Barney Ward, George Lindeman Jr, and a horse killer named Tommy Burns, among others, were each indicted for insurance fraud/wire fraud, involving the murder of horses for the insurance proceeds...." according to a report in *Chronicle of the Horse* in 2006. In addition, Ward was permanently banned from participating in or attending any horse shows by the United States Equestrian Federation, the governing body for most U.S. shows. In 2000, NY courts upheld the ban after Ward appealed it, according to the report, found at: www.chronicleforums.com/Forum/archive/index.php/t-76551.html.

In order to become an accomplished rider (and the more accomplished you become, the safer you are), you *must* do the work.

There is more to being a knight than a horse, sword and lance.

—Old proverb

Courage: One either comes with courage (the few), or learns it time and again (the many) through good training, good counsel and unremitting desire. Early on, when a new rider suddenly realizes that the animal is huge and strong and could do some serious damage, or even kill with one kick of a mighty hind leg, courage to press on is called for.

Courage, however, does not mean being foolhardy. Courage means making sure you've got everything possible set up in your favor, and then overcoming your residual fears and going ahead with it anyway.

It is courageous to get on a horse. Horses are big. Horses can move fast. Did we mention horses are big? For parents, especially, it is daunting to see their delicate daughter perched on top of an animal whose neck begins at the same height as the parent's nose. While it would be nice to be able to teach all junior riders on ponies, a good pony is a rare commodity, and so, size issues aside, juniors are often taught on horses.

Sometimes really, really big horses. "Mouse" was a Percheron cross used for "experienced" beginners at a Maryland farm. He was humongous. He was kind. He was well trained. He was the favorite horse of one of my 10-year-old beginners, to the point that she had t-shirts made with his name on them. She tacked poems about him to his stall. She rode him well.

Courage is throwing your heart up onto the horse, and letting your body follow. Later, courage is keeping a smile on your face in your first show when you know you really messed up and won't get a ribbon. It is congratulating your classmate, who won when you feel you should have. Courage is sportsmanship.

> **He that would venture nothing must not get on horseback.**
>
> —Spanish proverb

Courage is getting up and getting back on after a spill.

Although many trainers would disagree, courage is walking away from the sport when it doesn't serve you, nor you it. Once in love with horses, you will hunger for them forever.

Persistence: You may have seen the bumper sticker, "Happiness is a day in the saddle." However, misery can also be a day in the saddle. Sometimes, rider and horse just don't see eye to eye. The horse has had a bad night, or the rider had a bad night, or the weather doesn't suit one or the other, or someone is a little sore...and so on. One must be willing to ride through the bad days for the wonderful days to come, the ones described as, "Happiness is a day in the saddle."

Seeing the big picture: Riders learn to take in an enormous area around them and assess it for dangers to them and their horses. When they begin to show horses, they take in the essentials of the riding arena at a glance; they hold in mind the relative positions of other riders in the arena; they see what they must do to achieve their goals.

Taking care of details: The first time a rider falls off because, in the absence of a qualified instructor, the rider forgot to tighten the girth and the saddle slips, that rider learns to attend to the details. The first time the rider loses a beginner show ribbon for horsemanship due to forgetting to clean under the horse's tail, that rider learns to attend to the details. The first time a rider has a narrow escape from being scraped off when the horse runs into the barn because of an open arena gate, the rider learns to take care of ALL the details.

Selflessness and empathy: Watch *The Ballad of the Irish Horse,* a marvelous DVD from National Geographic. In it, a racehorse trainer with a house full of children and a field full of equines, says that, if one day the family has nothing to eat, they'll always feed the horses. That may be a peculiarly Irish attitude, or maybe not. It definitively describes the intense sense of responsibility and duty owners feel toward the magnificent beasts they care for.

Go to any lesson barn, hang around, and you will hear teenage girls discussing the fact that they could buy some more Abercrombie clothing for themselves with a recent windfall, or a new winter blanket for their horse. Ninety-nine times out of a hundred, the horse wins.

Watch a horsewoman around an injured horse. In fact, just watch an injured horse and see if you don't well up with sadness. There is nothing quite as potent for developing empathy as seeing misery in the eyes and body language of these enormous, noble beasts.

Taking one's self lightly: There's an old horseman's saying that, to a horse, a prince and a groom are exactly the same. The noblest thing in a barn is the horse, not the wealthy owner, not the gorgeous model posing for a fashion spread with the pretty animals. It's the horse. None of us is as noble as a horse; ask England's royal family. Princess Anne, an accomplished international competitor, has taken her spills on cross-country courses just like everyone else. She gets up and goes on. Watch riders in top shows who miss fences, crash and burn. They get up, dust off, take a courtesy jump, wave to the crowd, and likely as not, exit laughing at their own foibles. Or, perhaps the entire crowd erupts in laughter as an irrepressible stallion breaks wind in the air over every jump. What does the rider do? What *can* the rider do? She laughs, too.

> **A horse which stops dead just before a jump and thus propels its rider into a graceful arc provides a splendid excuse for general merriment.**
> —H.R.H., The Duke of Edinburgh

Enjoying the journey: Riders who chase money or accolades are called jockeys. The rest of us are chasing a variety of things, none of which says that the destination is more important than the ride.♥Some of us want exercise. Or, we want to be near horses and know how to interact with them. We want to be part of the beauty. We like games, such as jumping or camp games played on horseback. We want to be outdoors having fun. We don't care for the loneliness of the long-distance runner. We aren't built for football or field hockey. We love to dance, and having a horse for a partner would be fun. We love the smell of horses, the smell of leather, the smell of hotdogs at the concession stand at a horse show. We may love to win ribbons, too, but no one would endure the sacrifices—physical, emotional and financial—learning to ride requires in the hopes of getting an 89 cent ribbon after a day of hard work in the heat or cold, sun or rain. We ride because it is so much better than not riding.

Other things riders learn

A rider will learn to assess conditions relative to various tasks; is it too muggy to jump a horse today? Will my horse suffer and have a hard time cooling down and risk colic? Is it too cold? Will the ground injure his hoofs

---

♥ Please see previous footnote for an example of the exception to this rule.

or delicate legs? Many a rider has cried because, on a particular day, her intense desire to ride was overridden by her intense desire to care for her horse's needs first and foremost. So, riders also learn acceptance.

Riders learn that a relationship is not always fifty-fifty. With a horse, there are days when you'll give 100 percent. On the other hand, there are days when you will be such a bad rider that the horse will, quite literally, save your life. Why would a horse do this, if the horse has no loyalty and love like a dog? Well...hmmm...they might have some rudimentary altruism. Or they just might, as one of my own early trainers used to say, hate to lose their rider because it upsets the natural order of things from the horse's point of view. Horses don't like oddities in their environment, especially the sudden 'oddity' of a rider flying headlong off their back for what is, to the horse, no reason at all.

Riders also learn something about their place in the nature of things. Stories abound about the horse making the man, or the woman. England's Princess Anne, when learning to ride, was imperious and rude to her instructor. The instructor, so the story goes, sent the princess to sit on the manure pile until she had learned to behave with respect toward her teacher♥ and her horse, all with the Queen's blessing.

♥ Teacher and trainer are used interchangeably in this book, although many horsepeople will suggest that a trainer refers either to one who trains horses and not people, or to one who trains people and horses, or even just people, but is at a higher level than a mere teacher. Instructor is always used to refer to those who teach people, and not horses. However, an instructor may be a teacher when he or she is in the arena with a class, and a *trainer* when he or she is sitting atop a horse schooling, that is, training it. At base, all three words refer to a teacher, one who imparts knowledge to human beings and sometimes horses; instructors and trainers may have to get on a horse in a lesson and give it an 'attitude adjustment,' that is, refresh a horse's training in some way to make life easier for a student experiencing difficulties, thereby becoming "trainers".

> **They say princes learn no art truly, but the art of horsemanship. The reason is, the brave beast is no flatterer. He will throw a prince as soon as his groom.**
>
> —Ben Jonson, English writer (1572–1637)

Learning to ride has saved more than one delinquent wannabe from a life of crime. Horses, day in and day out, help riders develop self-confidence and self-control.

Riders learn that they must care for another creature before caring for themselves. Literally. Despite their size, horses have relatively delicate constitutions, and they must be cooled down and properly cared for before the rider gets any cooling down or cleaning off.

Riders learn love from horses. A dog teaches love by example. A horse teaches love by requiring riders to unconditionally love and care for the horse even when that horse might have vexed the rider to the point of tears. The most that the horse will give back is—maybe—a good ride next time out. Or maybe not. Riders learn to care for the idea of the horse, the spirit of the horse, the physical being of the horse. Riders learn unconditional love...and they learn that they are big enough to give that love without in the least diminishing themselves.

One can learn all this from riding any horse, not necessarily one's own. Indeed, for beginning riders, it is more beneficial to ride a variety of horses, such as one will find at a riding academy or lesson barn, in order to get to know some of the infinite nuances horses are capable of. Still, many beginning riders are understandably eager to have a horse of their own, one they can interact with at will.

Is it a good idea? Some trainers say absolutely not, while others are willing if the horse is right and the rider has the proper attitude. Some students have already bought the horse before they decide to take lessons; this is not an ideal situation, but whatever is, is. In this case, however, an experienced trainer is required to make it all come out all right for all concerned.

The best reason of all to ride

Most of us ride for the best reason of all: we love horses, and we want to be with them.

Little girls often yearn for horses before they are five. My youngest student ever was six; ordinarily, many barns won't begin lessons until a child is eight. Children need a certain amount of emotional maturity, size and strength, and ability to follow directions. By eight, most children can do a credible job of learning to ride with proper instruction. Younger ones? Almost never.

The father of the six-year-old convinced me that his child was willing and able, and he was right. She had been teasing for lessons since she was three.

The child was something of a prodigy. She understood instructions immediately, and was not the least bit intimidated by the horses.

The only time I knew she was so very young was when she came off; her howls were those of a very young child, not the same at all as those of older children. But she got up after only a few tears, and got back on. I came quickly to understand that with this child, the tears were not of fear, but disgust with herself for failing at something horse-related.

Some little boys yearn for horses, too, but fewer than girls. Adult women often have similar feelings to those of girls; adult men often want the exercise, or they want to master an art/sport they are unfamiliar with, or they want to join the females of the family on the trail or in the arena.

> **If I be once on horseback, I alight very unwillingly; for it is the seat I like best**.
> —Michel Eyquem de Montaigne, French writer
> (1533–1592)

In any case, love of the horse—its beauty, power, speed and sometimes spirit—are in the mix someplace. And, after the first glow of excitement, the initial fears, some minor discomfort as new muscles are found and strengthened, riders come to believe that, when mounted, they have the best seat in the house.

What we ride

A horse is a horse, of course, but what we call them will tell others how we ride them. In the English riding world, when one is talking about learning basic English riding skills, the sort of horse ridden is a hunter. The hunter may also jump, in which case he is a hunter-jumper. For brevity's sake, most riders will simply say they ride hunters.

A hunter is not a breed, but a type of horse. Thoroughbreds often make good hunters, as do Quarter Horses and Appaloosas. Irish hunters—a cross between an Irish Draught Horse and a Thoroughbred—make wonderful mounts, because they are bold, steady, intelligent and sturdy. But any breed that is not a gaited horse♥ (Tennessee Walkers, Standardbreds) can make a good hunter with the right training.

♥ A gaited horse has unique gaits that are different from the walk, trot and canter of most horses. Gaited horses are virtually all North American (Standardbred pacers and so on), except for the Icelandic horse. That horse offers a gait called a tölt, a four-beat running walk. These horses are unsuitable for jumping, and are generally used for other purposes, such as pack trains and riding over long and difficult distances.

14

The type of riding we do is called hunt seat. Dressage is a relative of hunt seat, and many dressage riders learned hunt seat first; some hunt seat riders learned dressage first. It is not much of a stretch for dressage riders to assume the hunt seat position, and vice versa, although there is a bit of snobbery one way or another about which seat is betters.   Answer: Neither. In my experience, learning some dressage helps refine hunt seat riders and horses used as hunters. By the same token, getting some hunt seat training makes dressage horses and riders bolder and more forgiving of imperfections.

Chapter Two: Is Riding a Dangerous Sport?

In a post-Christopher Reeve♥ universe, one must talk about injuries. Many people are afraid to ride because they fear injury. Parents are afraid to allow their children to ride because of the fear of injury.

Do they have any reason for their fear?

Yes, of course. But it shouldn't be paralyzing fear because, in some way, all sports are dangerous. *Living* is dangerous.

Still, it helps to know what the possibilities are so that you can make a rational assessment, and so that you will know that every safety procedure in this book—and every one you learn from *qualified trainers*—is worth following.

How dangerous is riding?

Between 1990 and 1992, the National Injury Surveillance System of the National Consumer Product Safety Commission developed figures based on records of injuries tended in hospital emergency rooms. The sports they selected for the study were golf, horseback riding, water skiing, tennis, snow skiing and bowling.

Their conclusion? In terms of head injuries, among the most worrisome of all injuries, golf takes the blue ribbon for the greatest number, with horseback riding second.

♥ Reeve played the title role in the 1978 movie, *Superman*. In 1995, he was paralyzed in a riding accident. He never blamed his horse, his trainer or the sport for his injury. Indeed, he was a hero to riders, appearing to thunderous applause as a guest speaker at the 2003 Washington International Horse Show. Reeve founded an organization to look for cures for spinal cord injuries and to offer other assistance to those with such injuries, regardless of the cause. Reeve died in 2004 from heart failure.

In terms of severity of the head injury, horseback riding failed to gain the top spot again: in snow skiing, almost half of the participants had injuries involving concussion, with horseback riding coming in at just over one fourth. Tennis and *bowling* were next, with a concussion percentage in the teens.

While one shouldn't assume that bowling is as dangerous as riding—after all, the bowling ball can't act on its own as a horse can—the fact that so innocuous a sport offers such abundant opportunity for injury is instructive.

The study noted that injuries to the mouth, face, eye and ear are most frequent in golf, water skiing and tennis, with horseback riding coming in fourth.

Horseback riding does not even win the injury contest in terms of fractures. While fractures are the most common type of injury in horseback riding, coming in at 30% of all riding injuries, snow skiing is not far behind, with 23% of all injuries in that sport being fractures. And *bowling* is third, at 17.5 percent. (Golf is almost fracture-free, with just 8.3% of its injuries diagnosed as fractures.)

If you are a parent trying to assess the danger of riding to your child, consider this: The same report noted that the greatest number of injured riders was the 25-44 year-old group. The number of fractures in that age group was three times the number in the 15-24 year-old group. The report concludes, "It can be postulated that the ages of 15-24 have the young bones, and although they have the greater number of [total] injuries each year, they have less fractures in the injury."♥ The report attributed this disparity to the fact, also, that older riders were both more experienced and *paid much more attention to safety issues (emphasis mine.)*

♥ The report can be found on a University of Vermont website at http://asci.uvm.edu/equine/law/amea/feb95nws.htm.

In 1994, the United States Pony Club (USPC) issued its *Accident Study*, which can also be found on the University of Vermont website[♥]. Its findings, because Pony Club is adamant about the use of protective headgear, note a decline in the number of head injuries in young riders. An earlier ten-year study showed a head injury percentage of 24.2 percent in USPC riders. For the first five years after use of ASTM/SEI helmets was required for junior riders, the injury percentage was 12.5 percent. By 1994, only 7.9% of USPC injuries were head injuries, an impressive statistic in favor of using ASTM/SEI helmets, a piece of equipment to be explained in Chapter Seven.

For Pony Clubbers, the most common type of injury was the bruise/abrasion at 41.3 percent, with sprain/muscle pull next at 17.3 percent, followed by "shook up" at 13.3 percent. The serious injuries of closed fractures and concussion were at 9.3 percent and 8 percent, respectively.

There were non-mounted accidents, as well. The most serious of these was caused by a lead rope being wrapped around a hand. When the horse misbehaved while being loaded onto a trailer, the rider could not get free of the rope and was killed.

First Rule of Rider Safety:

Never wind reins or lead ropes around your hands...or any other part of your body.

[♥] Ibid.

Second Rule of Rider Safety:

Never hook your fingers through any metal part of the bridle or saddle; make your hands as flat as possible for the task at hand when working with horses.

It bears repeating: Finding a qualified trainer or instructor is paramount. Avoiding unqualified personnel around horses—any unqualified personnel—is paramount. The notice below, also from the University of Vermont website, makes the case for having only qualified, knowledgeable equine instructors, trainers and barn managers assisting at a lesson barn where you ride or at your home paddock, for you and your children, better than any dry statistic ever could:

> The Fort-Worth Star-Telegram reported on January 15, 2004 that Garrett King, age 2, died after he was dragged through a pasture by a pony. The boy's baby sitter was moving horses from one pasture to another. The boy wanted to lead a horse, so the sitter wrapped the pony's lead rope around the boy's waist a couple of times and placed the end of it in his hands. The boy fell and spooked the horse. He suffered fatal head injuries as a result of being dragged. **♥**

It is impossible to emphasize this too much: **Find knowledgeable help for yourself or your children, and avoid being a sad statistic**. Instead, have a blast, and become one of the favored few, the horsey set. In the United States, according to the American Horse Council,

---

♥ Ibid.

1.9 million Americans own one or more horses; 4.3 million are involved in equine recreational activities. ♥

> **Informed opinion:** The term *qualified trainer or instructor* is an important one. Trainers and instructors who discount the dangers of riding and send beginners over fences too big for their skills, for example, are not qualified, no matter what their personal experience on horseback has been. Those who fail to insist on proper equipment, a conducive learning environment and attentive students are not qualified, no matter how many blue ribbons of their own hang on their walls. In short, if a trainer or instructor is reckless, disregards common sense, has a greater need to win than to keep students safe and allows disrespect or 'horseplay' in lessons or in the barn, that person is not qualified.

♥ Information developed by the National Ag Safety Database, which can be accessed at http://www.cdc.gov/nasd/docs/d000901-d001000/d000978/2.html

Chapter Three: Benefits of Riding

Winston Churchill, Prime Minister of England during World War II, is often quoted on his attitude toward horses. "There is something," he said, "about the outside of a horse that is good for the inside of a man."

Churchill was nothing if not wise and sane. Perhaps horses helped keep him so.

In any case, there is little doubt that riding can be a great stress reliever. Riding provides an opportunity for adults to let go their work, their family problems, even their personal problems for a little while. Riding demands one's attention, especially in the beginning when there is so much to learn. Stressed children, from those with learning disabilities to those with behavioral problems, can be helped by riding. Indeed, even children with serious developmental issues, from autism to profound developmental delays, are often helped by riding.

Therapeutic & Recreational Riding Center, Inc., (TRRC) in Glenwood, Maryland, lists an enormous array of challenges that are catered for at the facility. These include birth defects, and other issues that afflict both children and adults. NARHA-Certified♥ instructors teach riders with: muscular dystrophy, cerebral palsy, visual impairment, Down syndrome, mental retardation, autism, multiple sclerosis, spina bifida, emotional disabilities, brain injuries, spinal cord injuries, amputations, learning disabilities, attention deficit disorder, deafness, and cardiovascular accident/stroke.

TRRC is a Premier NARHA-accredited center, based on its extraordinary facilities and excellent and well-qualified hippotherapy staff. However, TRRC also caters to the needs of non-challenged individuals who simply

---

♥ NARHA stands for North American Riding for the Handicapped Association.

want an ultra-safe, ultra-low-key source of riding instruction with another staff of instructors qualified to teach riding to non-challenged students.

For example, one recent adult student at TRRC was a brilliant engineer who wanted to regain her strength after surgery, and decided riding would be just the thing. She had never ridden before, so her belief developed completely from her own research into the benefits of riding. She was right. I know this, partly because of my own decades-long research into the benefits of riding, and partly because I was her teacher. When she began, she could barely lift a gallon of milk. After several weeks, she was able to life heavy saddles onto the backs of large horses (she is a tall woman, and needs a big horse), and it went upward from there.

Private schools have been known to recommend that little boys with behavioral or self-esteem problems begin riding lessons. This, too, I have witnessed first-hand. Sometimes, a court will specify that a troubled and troublesome teenager begin riding, or at least working in a barn under supervision, and that works; this, too, I have seen first-hand.

Adults who have very stressful jobs often seek riding instruction. These people are often goal-oriented, and feel that the demands of learning to ride will give them a worthwhile target. Sometimes, they even begin to enjoy it!

Other adults take up the sport to spend time with one of their children, time they might otherwise fritter away or not spend at all.

On the other hand, adults (at least adult women) cry more often in lessons than any other group. If I had a nickel for every tear shed on horseback, I'd be a millionaire.

Riding, especially at the end of a taxing day, releases an enormous amount of bottled up energy. And, too, if the instructor has developed rapport with the student, it's almost a 'confessional' situation. The rider trusts the instructor, if the instructor does nothing to violate that trust. The rider, especially the adult rider, must trust the instructor in order to follow the frequent, and sometimes seemingly nonsensical (to a non-rider or beginning rider) instructions.

How many adults would sing various songs out loud while riding just because an instructor said to? And yet, one of the best ways to slow down a fast horse under a nervous rider and speed up a slow one under a lazy rider is to have each rider sing a song in the cadence that's required. "I'm in the mood for love," the old song from Our Gang's Alfalfa (fitting!) is great for slowing down a horse and rider, and often, the rider ends up in gales of laugher at the stupid song and stupid exercise, relaxing so much that the horse relaxes too, and slows down.

The lazy rider on the slow horse? Ask her to sing something Motown, something with a definite, and preferably faster, beat.

Riding is a great healer. It builds confidence and self-esteem, helps the emotionally delicate to get hold of themselves and situations, lets people express themselves in a relatively safe environment, gives them laughter (always healing) and joy.

The downside

Sometimes, riding produces emotional or physical pain. Taking the bad with the good, however, is a hallmark of sportsmanship, and horsemanship above all.

Even adult riders feel bad about losing a competition, even if it's just a local show and not a rated show. Riders might feel inadequate from time to time because they have trouble learning one or more skills. They might experience jealousy of better riders. They might develop an antipathy to a particular horse and dread being assigned that horse for a lesson.

Riding causes a certain amount of physical discomfort, even if one never falls off a horse.

For older girls and women, especially, there can be a great deal of discomfort while learning to trot. The legs might ache, as from any new exercise. But friction, as one pushes one's buttocks up from the saddle and forward toward the pommel, can cause pain and even abrasions in highly sensitive areas until the technique is properly learned and the muscles are sufficiently strong to support the effort without fail. (During this period, the rider should use the two-point position, which avoids contact with the saddle at the rider's sore points, until the abrasion calms down and the rider gets stronger. Riders have quit because their instructor was a man and they were too embarrassed to discuss the situation.

Women, especially those with hour-glass figures, need to invest in a sports bra, early on. And, as junior girls wend their way through puberty, the female adults around them will need to deal with a certain amount of embarrassment over the increasingly obvious signs of womanhood approaching; the girls will suddenly round their backs in an attempt not to display their bosom.

For boys and men, learning to post the trot, and, in addition, the jumping position, can require sports protective wear. Boys and men have quit because of this because their instructor was a woman, and they were too embarrassed to tell her.

Tall boots can make welts behind the knee, or rubs at the ankle. Short boots can allow the leathers holding the stirrups to bite painfully into the calf muscle. All these are easily overcome with bandages, time, and practice, but they are still part of every new rider's experience, almost without exception.

If a rider is assigned a 'hard puller,' a horse that likes to bear down on the reins and pull them through the rider's fingers, then rawness can develop between the ring finger and the middle finger on either or both hands.

Beginning riders can cause themselves pain by being overweight or out of shape. Contrary to popular belief, English riding is a *bona fide* sport and requires both muscle and dedication to be done well. Since it is more dangerous than tiddly winks, if you aren't willing to invest in your 'physical plant,' riding is not for you.

Flexibility is also a key component; yoga will develop this, as will many forms of dance.

Aerobics will help when it comes time to using body parts separately; kicking with the leg, squeezing the reins on one side, clucking, turning the shoulders and so on all at once.

An appreciation of art is also helpful; some riders view their own interaction with the horse in the arena as kinetic art.

The ability to let go of perfectionism is also required. One little girl—a very smart little girl who wanted to ride very, very much—could not conquer the trot. She posted wildly, oddly, in no sort of rhythm and all over the horse's back. It was a problem. Finally, in desperation, I asked her mother how she did in school. "Oh, Erin is an A student," her mother said. "She works so hard at everything. She just has to be the best."

AHA! A learning opportunity for the instructor! The child was trying too hard. She had to be encouraged to act dopey and lazy and let the horse do the work. Years later, when Erin was an accomplished rider, her mother told me she would sometimes hear Erin muttering, "Dopey, lazy bum" under her breath while riding.

You reap what you sow

In terms of benefits from riding, you will reap what you sow. If you allow yourself to become fully engaged in your equine 'experiment,' you will gain enormous emotional benefit, in addition to healthful exercise. This will be true whether you are an adult beginner or a child, or a mentally, physically or emotionally challenged individual of any age.

If you attempt to learn to ride without committing yourself to the best training and best experience you can find and afford, you are cheating only one person, and you know who that is.

Chapter Four: Equine Dollars and Sense

There is no part of your emotions horsemanship will leave alone. There is no part of your body that won't get some exercise. But your wallet will get some exercise as well.

While some think keeping a horse at home will be no more costly than the family dog, they are very mistaken. In fact, pleasure horses have been described as:

A moving lump on the landscape into which you pour money.

That's a very cynical viewpoint, especially to those who love horses. The cost of riding could better be described, perhaps, as

The Cost of a Little Bit of Heaven on Earth.

Still, it is expensive to ride, whether you keep a horse at home or board him. Figures developed by Allabouthorses.com put the cost of feeding one horse at home at more than $1,300 per year. That cost includes only hay (7,300 pounds), grain (700 pounds) and mineral salts (30 pounds). Nor does that take into account the added expense for extra hay in years when your pasture is inadequate to provide the forage the horse needs. Those years, you can almost bet that local hay producers will also have dry fields, and will have less to sell at higher prices. Or, you may even have to pay freight to have it shipped in from out of the area.

Also omitted from the equation is this: It is unwise to have just one horse. Horses are social animals—herd animals—and need others of their kind to be happy and healthy. So you can count on two horses, or a horse and a donkey.

While the donkey may be slightly less expensive, there will still be costs. Like the horse, the donkey—or second horse—will need inoculations, shoes or hoof trimming, worming, vet visits for injuries or illnesses, and, of course, bedding.♥ Bedding, like food and hay, is a constant cost. If the animals are simply field boarded, that cost is eliminated. But field-boarding horses in north temperate zones will be stressful to them in hard winters and you may find yourself literally protecting your investment by sending them to a boarding stable, at additional cost, for the duration of the awful weather. In southern temperate zones, summers may be too vicious for horses to remain always outside, and, again, if you do not have a building or stalls for them, you might end up sending them to a boarding stable for the hottest months.

If you field-board your horse, there is also the matter of fencing. Three- and four-board sturdy fence is required. Some people use much less expensive 'horse wire' fencing, a form of link that has four-inch segments supposedly much safer for horses than closer-knit wire. Not. A horse can snag a shoe in that wire when he kicks, pull off the shoe, maybe some hoof, and maybe do serious damage to soft—or hard—tissues of his leg. In addition, some localities require *double* board fence on all horse pastures near a public road. And most localities require a minimum acreage of paddock per horse, ranging from as

---

♥ Bedding is needed to protect the horse's delicate legs from hard ground or cement barn floors in their stalls, to absorb urine and contain feces within a small area, and to provide cushioning for the horse's heavy body. Field-boarded horses are afforded this sort of protection by grass and the (usually) softer earth outside, not packed down as earth in a stall becomes.

little as one acre per two horses, to five acres for each horse. Fencing, no matter where you live, will add lots of cost.

Unless you want trouble from the humane movement—not to mention harming your "best friend"—you will abandon any thoughts of keeping your horse always stabled except for riding, thereby eliminating or greatly reducing fencing costs.

Additional costs, of course, will be training for you and possibly for your horse, if there are things he needs to know and doesn't. Not all horse trainers are created equal, and some produce horses that lack essential experience in some area of equine pleasure mount work.

Keeping a horse at home? Or on board?

If you only want to own one horse, it will be more convenient and arguably almost as cost-effective, to keep him on full board at a lesson barn. Fees range from about $150 a month for field board to a low of about $300 for stall/field board to $800 *or more* per month for stall/field board. The advantage to you is that you do not have to install fencing, you do not have to do all the daily chores involved in horse care (feeding and watering and haying, cleaning stalls and rebedding them, turning the horse out and bringing him in, blanketing and unblanketing in winter, applying fly spray before turnout in summer.) You only need to write a check.

Other advantages to boarding are, usually, access to good arenas for hacking and training, wash stalls with hot and cold water for bathing the horse, groomed and relatively safe fields for a change of pace, camaraderie for you and for your horse, and professional help as you learn to ride and handle and care for horses. While you will pay for your riding lessons in addition to board fees, what you can learn about horses and horse care, and sometimes even riding, from experienced barn managers is worth its weight in horseflesh. And that information is free for the asking. Just hang around and respectfully ask questions.

The average board fee in the United States is about $300 per month, for a yearly total of $3,600. That will include feed, hay and bedding. It will not ordinarily include salt blocks or worming, although some barns do add those to their basic services. Some barns will charge extra for blanketing. Virtually all barns will charge for administering medicine; they may charge to hold the horse when he needs to be seen by the vet, whether for the routine yearly shots or because of illness or injury. Some barns will require monthly worming. Virtually all will require a half-dozen inoculations each year (especially rabies and tetanus) and a negative Coggins.

Whether you field-board your horse at home or keep him in the most expensive barn in your area, you'll have farrier costs as well. Shoes will cost anywhere from $45 a shoeing for two front shoes only, to $100+ for four shoes, to well over that for orthopedic shoeing. Older horses will almost always require four shoes, and some horses, both young and old, will require special shoes to cope with less than perfect conformation or other issues that affect their way of going or health. Horses need shoes about eight times a year. Allabouthorses.com estimates that owners spend an average of $345 per year for their horse's shoes.

Horse haberdashery

Your horse needs clothing, too. Horses need blankets in winter in cold climates, sunsheets in summer in warm climates, fly sheets in any climate, coolers in any climate. A cooler is a blanket meant to keep the horse from getting chilled as his wet fur dries after a hard ride. Costs can range from $65 or so for discount horsewear to a few hundred for the most popular, durable and fashionable blankets from a bevy of foreign manufacturers.

Your horse will also need basic equipment, at least a saddle that fits both your horse and you well, and a bridle. A new close contact (English) saddle of reasonable quality will be about $1,000, with stirrup irons, stirrup leathers and girth. A couple of saddle pads, to allow for washing, will be another $50 to $100. A complete bridle (including reins) will be a minimum of $80; adding at least one bit will add about $30. As time goes on, and you and your horse become more accomplished (or your horse develops a physical or attitudinal problem), you may need to change bits, change bridle styles, or add a second set of reins. Your horse's conformation may require use of a breastplate to keep the saddle in the proper position; if your mount is a pony, it may require a crupper to keep the saddle properly situated. Your horse may require some sort of protective boot for his ankles, depending on his way of going. Add about another $200 to your budget for miscellaneous equipment costs.

Rider couture

You, too, will need clothing. You'll need an ASTM/SEI helmet (figure $100 for a good one), breeches (from about $40 on sale to well over $200), a selection of shirts to wear for lessons (a few polos or tees, figure $50 to $75), and tall boots ($125 at the low, off the rack, for leather), or paddock boots ($65 and up) and chaps ($75 off the rack, on sale, to a couple hundred for custom-made.) Ten bucks for scrunchies. Twenty-five for gloves for winter. And the cost of a down vest, or warm, light, short jacket suitable for riding if nothing in your closet will serve.

Next to your horse, you're a cheap date!

Chapter Five: Your Kingdom for a Horse?

If you are a beginner rider, and you want to buy a horse, you really need only one bit of advice: **Don't.** Or at least, wait until you've ridden enough horses to know what type of horse you like to ride—big, small, fast, slow, bony, fat, willing, cantankerous. Really? Yup. There are riders who prefer a horse with 'tude.

> **Informed opinion:** Often, barn owners are so eager to fill stalls with paying customers that they will encourage the purchase of unsuitable horses. It is not for nothing that the phrase is often used regarding any sort of horse trading, "When you shake his hand, count your fingers." Be sure your advisor has your best interests in mind.

Your first horse

When you are ready, be patient until the right horse comes along. Take a trusted advisor with you when you look, and never buy a horse you haven't ridden more than once. Horses are different on different days. Horses can be drugged. Horses can be 'quick fixed' to perform well for you, reverting to bad habits as soon as the memory of the recent 'attitude adjustment' wears off.

If you are considering buying a horse early in your riding career, here are some factors to consider:

- Horse's age
- Horse's size
- Horse's training
- Horse's health
- Horse's temperament
- Horse's breed

Horse's age

If you are a beginning rider, avoid a young horse. Young horses, even of the calmest breeds, can get excited at the wrong time. Like a young human, they lack experience of the world, and can be unsettled by things that are normal to those who've been around a bit. How young is too young? Certainly any horse under three is too young. While race trainers put horses on the racetrack at under two years of age, those horses are expected to do only one thing, run in an enclosed oval for a specified distance, and woe betide even experienced jockeys who try to get them to do anything else.

If you mean to jump the horse, it should be at least three and preferably four before being jumped. As in young mammals of any sort, the cartilage and bones of young animals is elastic, so elastic that it can be stretched in hurtful ways, or used in such a way that bones are also put at risk.

So, any horse you buy to ride should be at least, realistically, four years old.

Be aware, though, that four does not necessarily mean four in the equine world. For matters of convenience when assigning racehorses to age classes, every Thoroughbred in the country is considered to have a birthday on January 1, whether the horse was foaled in January or May. Obviously, those born closer to January 1 are actually older than the May foals, and therefore have an advantage at the track, being older, better developed, more mentally mature, and stronger. Race trainers like early foals; pleasure riders need not be concerned with that issue, just with finding a horse—Thoroughbred or other—that is actually four years old *by the calendar,* not by racehorse reckoning.

However, a young Thoroughbred of riding age may not be the best breed for a new rider to buy, an issue that will be dealt with below.

Age can work against a new rider in another way, also.

Let's say the new rider finds the perfect horse, and that horse is 12 years old. It is calm, well-trained, of a size and temperament that appeal to the rider, and the horse is even the perfect color, the dapple gray the rider had always dreamed about. Listen to this conversation:

Trainer: I don't think you should buy him. He's too old.

Rider: But he's beautiful, and he should be able to work for me for at least eight or ten years, right? I mean, I wouldn't retire him before age 22 or so if he were healthy, right?

Trainer: Yes, that's true. But think about this. You don't know what injuries he may have already had at that age, and a vet check won't reveal everything.

Rider: No, but I'm willing to take the chance. He's so beautiful!

Trainer: Beauty is as beauty does.

Rider: But he is kind. I almost fell off him and he slowed down. He saved me!

Trainer: I told you, horses get freaked out when they lose a rider, so a lot of them try to prevent it for their own peace of mind. It is a good quality in a horse for you. But still....you shouldn't buy him.

Rider: Why, for heaven's sake?

Trainer: Because, when you are ready to jump 3-foot fences and compete in the show ring with the other amateur owners, he will be too old to do that job for you. He will be, by that time, best served by jumping smaller fences and toting around beginners trying to learn—like you. Like you right now. See what I mean? You will surpass the capacity of your horse. So look for a horse that is about six now, and then you'll have several years together, barring injury, when you are capable of doing the same kind of riding and jumping.

Horse's size

Do not buy a 17–hand horse for a ten-year-old rider; do not buy a 15–hand horse for a tall adult. For starters, the ten-year-old will have a hard time mounting a huge horse, and the adult will put too much weight on the smaller animal.

Suitability is another issue. In the hunter show ring, especially, horses and riders need to be suited to each other, to present an attractive picture. A tiny girl on a monstrous horse looks odd; a large adult on a tiny horse looks even worse, plus it appears cruel to the horse.

In addition, adults are not allowed to show ponies in rated shows; often, junior riders are not allowed to show anything but ponies, although this is not a hard and fast rule, as long as the proportions are in sync. After all, some 12-year-old girls are 5'8" and would be too big even for large ponies and must, therefore, ride and show horses.

Once you've determined if you are a pony rider or a horse rider, the hard work of finding a truly proportionate horse begins. One way to do this is to sit on a number of possibilities and have a reliable trainer assess the picture.

What if you are exactly the same height as your friend? Could you not be well served by the same horses and buy one just like hers? Maybe not. My own horse is quite large, 16 h., 2 in. He's bulky, as well; a real man's horse. However, he fits me for two reasons. First, I have very large thighs (probably from early ballet and later horses), so they cover some of his bulk. Second, I have had theatrical training, which gives me a certain presence on the horse. So, even though I am only 5'5", the horse fits me. He also fits tall men. But he made my friend who is just my height, but who has slender legs and is very shy, look like a fly on a bed sheet. That's fine if all you want to do is hacks and trail rides. If you want to show horses, though, it pays to get the picture right.

About adults and jumping: Almost every adult beginner I have ever taught has said they didn't want to jump and certainly didn't want to show horses. They all claimed they only wanted to learn how to ride so they could go trail riding in greater comfort. Or they wanted to know what their riding children were experiencing. However, without exception, when I told them their skills indicated that they were ready to jump, not a single one declined. Not one. (And one, right after her first jump and with a huge smile on her face, yelled out, "Ooooh, it's just like flying!" She bought a horse four months later.) Of those, more than half ended up riding in shows for ribbons and having a great old time.

Horse's training

Of all the equine "must haves", training is the absolute. The people who jumped onto the untrained horses in *Lonesome Dove* were stuntmen—specifically, equine stuntmen. You're not. So, you'll need a horse that's trained, and preferably one that's trained well to do what you want it to do. Since it generally takes at least a couple of years to train a horse to all the basics, insisting on a trained horse will help you get the age right as well.

A horse for a beginner should do all the following reliably, whether or not an experienced rider is riding/handling the horse:

Stand for mounting without moving.

Walk forward from a light kick and certainly from leg pressure (that is to say, the horse should accept a light kick, as most beginners kick more often than press for quite a while).

Trot with harder leg pressure or harder light kicks and/or a cluck.

Canter on the proper lead when the rider asks (pressing or light kick) with the outside leg behind the girth, regardless of what the rider is doing with his or her hands.

Halt (stop) when the rider pulls back on the reins, either tactfully or not.

Stand for dismount without moving.

Jump over an 18-inch fence from the trot with the rider in two-point (jumping) position as long as the rider has aimed the horse toward the jump properly. The horse should trot away after the jump unless asked to canter.

Informed opinion: Many school horses automatically canter off after a jump, and many instructors believe this is best. But a beginner rider who is going to work on his or her own would be better served by a horse that trotted away from jumps unless specifically asked to canter. Even in riding school situations, horses that automatically canter have limited use; they are too bold for timid beginner riders. And, if they canter automatically, the rider cannot be taught how to ask for the canter after a jump, a useful skill for lazy or less well-trained horses the rider might later encounter.

Horse's health

A horse that's more than a couple of years old will be very likely to have some signs of injury, and even a bit of wear and tear. A horse of about six, the age I recommend for beginners (within reason and the bounds of intelligent assessment), will almost certainly have some signs of wear and tear. Unfortunately, some trainers and owners and veterinarians think the least sign of aging is reason 'not to pass' the horse. In fact, whether a horse 'passes the vet' is up to the owner and the trainer, not the vet. The vet's job is to find and disclose all the dings and dents; it is not to tell the purchaser don't buy him or do buy him. That decision is for the rider and the trainer together.

Still, if you and your trainer have found a suitable horse, it would not be wise to buy him without input from an equine veterinarian.

A vet-check generally costs about $125, or a little more, and involves the vet giving the horse a general physical, including: palpating its belly, listening to heart and lungs, taking its temperature, looking for signs of disease or injury in its eyes and mouth, ascertaining its age by various physical signs such as the grooves in its teeth (Galvayne's grooves), and, very importantly, assessing its legs and how it moves. The vet will have someone jog the horse—lead it at a walk and then a trot—in both directions. And she may want to see it lunged—that is, asked to canter on a 25-foot lead. If she sees something in the horse's gait she doesn't like, she will do a flexion test; she will hold the lower part of the leg in question in a cocked position for a few minutes and then assess how long it takes the horse to recover from the 'flexing' and resume a normal gait when it trots away.

If she is still not satisfied, she may ask if you want to go ahead with a portable x-ray, which will, of course, add cost and also time as vets do not carry the equipment with them as a rule and must make a special trip.

A vet will not tell you, "Do not buy this horse," or "Do buy this horse." She will describe her findings. A good vet will also have asked you what you plan to do with the horse in terms of riding and sport, and what your own capabilities are. Then she will tell you the probable effect of the horse's condition, whether perfect or compromised in some way, on those things. Then it will be up to you to make the buy decision; again, having a trustworthy, experienced rider/trainer with you is very, very valuable to help properly interpret what the vet is telling you.

There are, of course, some absolutes, but very few. If the horse has a metal plate in its leg and you intend on jumping the horse, don't buy it. If you're positive you only want to trail ride, then that horse might be a contender for your love and dollars. If the horse requires four people to hold it on the ground, using a twitch, for its temperature to be taken, don't buy it. If the horse is for sale because it kicked its previous owner in the head, don't buy it. While such a horse may not be a rogue, it will require an experienced rider/handler. You would be wise not to trust it. You can't know why it kicked that way, handler idiocy or equine distress. Or maybe it's a rogue.

These are not all of the 'don't buy' situations (there are more in the next section). But they should get you thinking about what you can—and should—handle in terms of taking on the responsibility and, one hopes, the pleasure of horse ownership.

Horse's temperament

When you're buying a horse, it will pay you to think like a horse trader. How's that? Hmmm...well, recall the 'count your fingers' instructions? Like that. To be kind, just think of it as 'trust your neighbors, but lock the door.' When you look at a horse in its home arena—barn, field, riding ring—it will be as calm as it ever is. How will it be in new surroundings? And how will it be if, in fact, it has been given one of several calmative compounds on the market and that compound wears off? Especially for a beginning rider, a calm and placid temperament is paramount.

So, try the horse out in its own backyard, but also insist that you be allowed to try it at your own place—your home if you have equine facilities, or whatever boarding stable you have chosen. Make the trial period at least 33 days, and offer to pay a lease fee for the privilege; if the owner balks, keep looking. (Why that long? Because if the seller is going to drug the horse, it takes 30 days for some painkilling and/or calming horse medicines to fully wear off. You need to see how the horse is when it is fully itself. And you need for your advisor or trainer to see that as well.)

If the horse has stall manners that require humans to enter the stall with a 2x4, brandishing same, don't buy it. If it bites, don't buy it. If it rears, don't buy it. If it is visibly lame doing its usual work during a month-long tryout, don't buy it. If it seems sweet natured, but has a reputation in the area as a rogue, don't buy it; it has probably been drugged. There are drugs that don't wear off for about 30 days, just enough time for unsuspecting buyers to be had; did I mention the part about counting fingers?

If it disrespects humans, don't buy it. Paramount among temperament faults to avoid is disrespect for humans. A few horses would truly just as soon run over you as look at you. Some of them are fine performers, and perfectly amenable to doing what you wish, unless it conflicts with what they wish.

If Old Buck is truly desirable, and there actually is along line of people waiting to buy him, then Old Buck is the rare exception in the pleasure–horse world. There is only one certainty in looking for a horse; there is always another one, perhaps even better than the first one you considered.

Warning! Some years ago, a friend purchased a horse for her teenage daughter. The horse was supposed to be an Appaloosa, but of course, no papers proving this were offered. The horse was a solid light gray, almost white. Appaloosas can be non-spotted, but usually, they are dark. The horse did have the bone of the Appaloosa, and he wasn't prone to blowing up when faced with strange situations with a rider on his back.

The problem was, sometimes he got just a bit hot, even for the teen who was a good, advanced rider. She would get on anyway, but when her mother rode the horse, when the teen was away or too busy with school, it was better to longe the horse.

Problem: The horse didn't like being longed. In fact, although she was an experienced rider (but a petite woman), the thought of longing that horse scared the mother to pieces. One day, I offered to do the job for her, forgetting that people are reluctant to tell others all the problems with their animals.

I was preparing the longe line, always recalling, naturally, not to get it wrapped around my hands or body in any way. Still, I did engage in a stupid horse trick: I had already hooked the longe line to the horse's halter, removing his familiar lead line, before I prepared the longe line which had been left on the ground in a mess. (NEVER leave equipment around; it destroys the equipment over time, not to mention posing a hazard for riders and trainers.)

While I was preparing the longe line, I looked away for just a second. The horse—horses are opportunists!—decided to take advantage of me. When I looked back at him, I realized he was either going to bolt or charge: I preferred bolting. And that's exactly what he did. I tossed the longe line away as fast as I could, but the donut on its end came up and caught my ring finger and pinky and bent them back to my wrist. They ballooned to the size of sausages, and I'm quite sure every tendon was blown. To this day, those fingers are crooked on my hand, don't close as well as all my other fingers, and generally show the signs—six years later—of my stupid horse trick.

There are three lessons here.

Lesson one: Even trainers can have a momentary lapse, and, as with beginners, they will suffer the consequences.

Lesson two: If more than one person in a family is going to ride the horse, it needs to be appropriate for all.

When the incident was over, and I was running to the barn for cold water, having grabbed a lead rope and slung that horse into an open paddock, the mother said, "Oh, our vet told us when we bought that horse that he was the kind that could never be trusted with a longe, or anything else he viewed as an insult."

Lesson three: Sometimes, although a vet will not say buy or don't buy, they will offer extremely useful information.

> **Informed opinion:** To my mind, that horse did not need to be owned by any sort of pleasure rider of any age or any experience. He was not trustworthy, and he could kill someone if he charged.

Horses must respect human space; if they don't, then they don't need to breed (who can tell if it's their training or their intrinsic self that causes this?) and they don't need to be in situations where they can damage or kill humans, or, for that matter, dogs or other horses. A horse that disrespects a human's space is, pure and simple, a rogue. And, despite courting outcries from the humane world, I do think they should be euthanized, unless they can find work that absolutely keeps them away from anyone who might be abused by their intractable nature.

Eventually, the mother and daughter sold the horse.

Horse's breed

Any breed is fine, really. As long as the factors above are all in order, then any breed is fine. It usually happens that a Thoroughbred isn't the first horse; most Thoroughbreds have raced, or at least were bred for racing, and are both too fast and too eager to run for beginners. But there are exceptions.

Quarter Horses often serve, although they can be so stubborn that they bring great frustration to beginners, unless they have been very well trained and are over their stubborn baby years; some people believe a Quarter Horse is not mentally mature until age ten.

Appendix Quarter Horses, those crossed with Thoroughbreds, are often good first horses, as long as they combine the willingness of a Thoroughbred with the steadiness of a Quarter Horse.

Some Warmbloods can work (Hanoverians, Lippizaners, etc.), although they are so highly bred and so valuable in the dressage show ring that it is unlikely a beginner rider would find one of the proper age and size (not huge) to serve the purpose.

Arabians...OK. There is an exception to every rule. I would absolutely, positively not consider an Arabian for a beginner rider. They are often flighty. They can be incredibly ignorant when it comes to jumping, giving even small jumps lots of 'air' and often leaving long—that is, leaving out a stride and making the air time too long for beginners, not to mention the possibility of unseating the unprepared rider. They are generally small, often too small to look good under a large adult. They can be tyrants in their stalls. And, for the hunter show ring, their carriage is all wrong, with heads held too high, tails both held and set too high, and gaits that are too ground-covering for horses their size.

Appaloosas are often considered to be spotted Quarter Horses. In fact, they are a bit different, with a little more interest in working than Quarter Horses. Some of them are very smart and easy to train. On the other hand, the dumbest horse I've ever met was an Appaloosa. Still, he was a great—if not challenging—school horse. Like riding a safe tank; no spills, but no thrills either.

Morgan horses are usually calm and steady. Bred to do a variety of tasks—pulling a plow on weekdays, pulling the family buggy to church, being ridden to town—they are versatile. Often, however, they are not handy jumpers, as their backs can tend to be long, giving quite a bouncy ride over a fence. Still, some are 'short coupled' and they are, possibly as much as the Quarter Horse, a truly American breed.

Draft horse crosses, as long as they have some age on them and were polite as field hunters—which most of them start out as because of their size, steadiness and ability to go forward with no nonsense—can make nice horses for sizeable beginners. A common cross in the United States is Percheron and Thoroughbred. An Irish Hunter is a cross between any of the prevalent heavy breeds in that nation (Shires, for one) and Thoroughbreds, and quite a few have been imported and sometimes become available as pleasure mounts; many are used by Grand Prix riders and very serious hunt club members.

All the 'other' breeds—Haflingers, Akhal-Tekes, and other less prevalent horse breeds—are possible, or impossible, depending on what they have been bred and/or trained to do. If you could afford a nice Akhal-Teke, you'd not go far wrong. The real old desert horse, they are easy keepers, have nice strides, are incredible to look at—gleaming red-gold—and usually have placid temperaments no Arabian ever considered displaying. The first stallion whose field I invaded during mating season was an Akhal-Teke, and all he did was trot over and look for a treat. Later that day, I rode him and he was a perfect gentleman. At the time, I was not a trainer, and was, in fact, intimidated until the breeder proved to me the wonders of the breed. With so few around, however, they are extremely expensive but, if you can afford one, worth every penny.

Do not buy a horse for its color. Palominos are striking. Grays are elegant. Chestnuts can gleam in the sun. Paints are cute. But none of that matters in your first 'learning to ride' horse. What matters is the forgiving temperament, and complete training. (No, Palomino is not a breed, it's a color, a bright sand color, and it can occur in several breeds.)

Warning! Any generalization made about horses will be proven wrong sooner or later. But take the generalizations to heart anyway, because they will work 90 percent of the time, and at this point, you have no personal experience to draw on. But don't completely rule out exceptions, either, as long as you get good advice about those exceptions.

Horse's size

Horses are measured in hands, and a hand is four inches. So a fifteen-hand horse is five feet high at the withers.

The withers is the place where his backbone becomes neck bone and is a little raised bump where you can feel the vertebrae quite well with your fingers.

If you are an adult buying the horse, you will need to consider two things; your height and your weight. (Your weight will also influence which breed you should buy; even though a Thoroughbred may be tall, they are generally fine-boned and 'slab-sided' and could have trouble carrying the weight of a man of 6 feet and 210 pounds, for example. A large man would want to consider a very large, 16+-hand Quarter Horse, or a Warmblood (quite bulky horses) or, if he is really heavy, a draft horse cross. These are most often Percherons or Clydesdales crossed with Thoroughbreds.

A height of 16 hands is still considered tall for a Quarter Horse, as they are usually found at about 15.2 hands. But some Quarter Horses have been bred for racing, and those tend to be taller and generally more Thoroughbred-like in their conformation. But they still behave like the old-fashioned Quarter Horse type. They can run quite fast for short distances, but they are often lazy (problematical) as well a placid (desirable in a beginner horse.)

For most women between 5'3" and about 5'6", a horse of about 15 hands to 15.3 hands or so is adequate. Women under 5'3" are not too big for all but the smallest small ponies, as far as carrying them, as long as the woman's weight is in proportion to height. But an adult woman cannot show a pony in horse shows, so if she intends to show, then she should not buy a pony, but rather, a small horse.

Junior riders, those who have not reached their 18th birthday, can show ponies. But, of course, most girls who are 14 or so have reached most of their adult height and would be a problem for a small pony to carry, or even some medium ponies. And boys, too, will shoot up in time—although possibly later than girls—and outgrow their horse.

That's why, when buying a pony for a child to ride and especially to show, it is often wise to buy a bulky medium or a large pony so the child can continue to show that pony all the years until he or she is no longer a junior rider. Little kids do look cute on little ponies, but that choice should be an option only if you plan on buying new ponies each time the child outgrows one. And then there's the bonding issue to contend with; families often end up with more ponies at home or on board than they intended because they cannot bear to sell the outgrown ponies that have become family members by then, especially if the pony 'taught' the child to ride.

A pony is any horse that measures less than 14.2 hands at the withers. They can be of any breed.

About the Connemara: A Connemara Pony is not a pony *per se*, but a small, sturdy horse from the west of Ireland. These are now bred in the U.S. as well, and can be a good choice for beginning riders, as long as they are well trained and old enough. Because they are a very tough breed, they can carry a larger person than one might suppose at first.

The price of a horse

The price of a horse can range from a very low point of $500 for an older horse without many useful years left or for a horse with serious injuries, to multiple thousands for fine horses of any popular breed used for hunt seat: Thoroughbreds, Quarter Horses, Morgans, Friesians, European Warmbloods, and the 'niche' breeds, such as Akhal-Tekes, a breed which sells for a minimum of $25,000.

For a first pleasure horse, unless you know you need one with the talent and physical refinement to show in rated (that is, upper level) shows, you should be able to find a suitable horse for between $2,500 and $7,500. For a good pony, you might pay a bit more. For a horse or pony that is very plain—a chestnut with no markings, for example—you might pay a bit less. For a horse with a lot of 'chrome,' that is, a star on his forehead and four white socks, you might pay a bit more. You might get a bargain if you can offer a good home to the beloved horse of someone who is moving overseas and cannot take the horse. You might get a bargain if a family cannot support the child's pony after the child has moved on to horses. If a horse is too cheap next to others of its type, size, breed, age and training, be careful. There may be temperament issues, or concealed injuries.

Before you look at horses in person, visit horse sales websites and sections of local publications and equine publications that list horses for sale. You can do the homework on 'comparables' in horses just as you would to find out the correct price point to expect for the sort of house you want to buy.

Horses that are fully trained, or in hunt-seat parlance 'made', are generally between five and ten years old. At those ages, they will command the highest prices likely to be paid for them in their lives (except if they are fancy show horses and win a lot in the next few years, in which case the price can go up.) But if you are a green—that is, inexperienced—rider, you MUST have a fully trained, calm, forgiving horse or pony.

Remember, too, that the cost of the horse is not the same as the price of the horse. Unless you buy a supremely expensive horse and keep him in your backyard, you will spend infinitely more during the horse's life on his upkeep (board, shoes, vet fees, hauling to shows or trail rides or hunts, equipment for horse and rider, travel expenses, insurance) than on the horse itself.

Seek good advice

When you look for a horse, it would be best to take an experienced horsewoman or horseman with you. Have that person ride the horse and tell you whether it would be suitable before you get on. But be sure the advisor is reputable and knowledgeable and not prone to taking horses for granted. One of my adult beginner students bought a horse on the advice of a life-long rider who was her neighbor and claimed to know horses. My student was tossed by that horse at least 100 times in the first year she owned him. Why? The horse was a willful, green Thoroughbred, and the rider had never—that's NEVER—ridden before. She came for lessons after that, and was just lucky she hadn't gotten seriously hurt in the time before lessons, and was plucky enough to continue with horses anyway. No one needs to go through that.

If you have already bought a horse...

You might, of course, have already bought a horse. If it's suitable, stick with it. If it's not—either right now or sometime in the future—think about leasing it to someone it is right for and leasing or buying another for yourself. Indeed, if you are a beginner rider, and you want access to a horse more often than your weekly lesson (and let's face it, the more time you spend in the saddle, the quicker you'll get proficient), think about a short-term lease of a suitable horse. Then, as you advance, you can move up to leasing a more demanding horse.

Chapter Six: Finding Lessons

One of the prime considerations in learning to ride should be safety; horses are huge, powerful animals with minds of their own. Trying to learn to ride without the assistance of someone who is skilled at interpreting what both horses and riders require, and making those requirements mesh most of the time, is idiocy, pure and simple.

Before going on, please drop any idea you might have that riding can ever be 100% safe, or that there is a trainer anywhere in the universe who will never make a mistake. If you are the sort who likes to sue others over their mistakes—but one is certain, of course, you wouldn't like being sued over yours—please do everyone a favor and find another sport. A sport that doesn't involve physical risk. Tiddly winks might be a good bet.

That having been said, how do you go about finding a competent riding academy or teacher? In English equine sport, there is virtually no credible certification organization in the United States (in Great Britain, there is the British Horse Society, which both trains and certifies teachers and trainers at all levels.) And, while most of us can tell if a piano teacher knows one note from another simply by listening, very few people have any experience of what good horsemanship is, never mind whether it is being taught safely and well.

Not much help

Below is a description of a Level One instructor from the CHA website. [*]

A CHA first-level instructor is:

---

[*] http://www.cha-ahse.org/cert.htm#standard.

"Qualified to provide foundational instruction to beginners, with a strong emphasis on safety and group control; candidates must demonstrate ability in ground handling, mounting, correct position and control at walk-trot."

This means that the candidate must be able to tack up and lead a horse, get on the horse, sit on the horse properly, and be able to direct and stop the horse while walking or trotting.

But what happens if a horse in a lesson, carrying a beginner, decides to canter? The instructor, under these guidelines, need not know how to ride this natural gait herself, never mind instruct a student who is on the horse how to ride the canter to a stop, *ASAP*. Remember, horses have brains of their own.

In the case of beginning riders, the horse knows more than the rider; certainly, the instructor should know as much as the horse, and preferably more. The CHA standards don't call for that, and yet, many a riding academy will boast of its lower level "certified" instructors.

Informed opinion: The most commonly noted certification body in the United States is the Certified Horsemanship Association (CHA). Quite frankly, its standards are minimal. And, if one is looking for instruction and is a beginner, one might well decide a trainer with a first or second level certification would suffice. In my opinion, it doesn't. Until a teacher/rider is accomplished in both practice and theory to an advanced level, he or she is likely to get riders in trouble because of limited knowledge. Even beginners—no, *especially* beginners—need instruction from those with more breadth and depth of knowledge than described in the CHA minimum standards.

Here's an analogy to further explain the problem with this limited 'certification': Do you really want to get on a commercial airplane flown by a lower level pilot who knows how to take off, fly straight and land as long as the weather is fine and the mechanicals are perfect? Probably not. No one can guarantee perfect weather and mechanics that won't ever develop a glitch. Just so for horses.

Apply discernment to your quest

If you are determined to seek a barn with CHA certification, look for an academy with Level Four CHA instructors or CHA Master Instructors. And even then, be skeptical. The instructors have demonstrated abilities defined by the CHA and judged by the CHA. There is no way standards can be applied to the equine world in the same way standards can be applied to airplane pilots. Airplane engines don't have brains. Horses do.

Avoid teaching prima donnas

Here's another problem: In the larger, non-CHA world of horses, many trainers and teachers with advanced knowledge think they are above teaching beginners. However, advanced teachers and trainers who understand how people acquire physical skills, as well as understanding what the future of the sport requires, will be happy to teach beginners. Their greater knowledge will contribute to greater safety, and they are also ensuring a stream of well-taught riders to move up into the more advanced levels.

Informed opinion: Until there is some organization with the stringency of the British Horse Society available to certify instructors in the United States, you'll be better off looking for an extremely experienced instructor, one who has ridden enough horses, competed in enough shows, and handled enough breeds to have a reasonable body of experience that can be used to keep students safe and learning proper riding technique. Look for one who, in addition to all that, is able to communicate instructions to riders clearly and forcefully at all times so that, in an emergency situation (runaway horse, sudden upheaval near the arena that upsets horses, and so on) the instructions will be likely to be heard and followed.

How to find competent instructors

Use CHA certification only as a starting point in your quest for good instruction, not as a recommendation in and of itself.

If you happen upon a British Horse Society-certified instructor, that's different. While competency levels in that program are also graduated, achieving even the lowest level requires intensive immersion in all things equine. The BHS requires rigorous training and virtual slave labor in the equine world to achieve any of its certification levels. Despite that, or because of it, British Horse Society (BHS) certification is avidly sought by horse sports lovers, and is rightly highly regarded by those wishing to learn the sport. If you find a BHS certified instructor in the United States, give him or her a good, hard look because that teacher is likely to rise to the top of your list of possible teachers. (Find more specific information about BHS levels on their website, at www.bhs.org.uk.)

If you live in the vicinity of a college offering equine studies (and there are only a dozen or so nationwide), call and ask their head instructor to recommend a local riding academy or lesson barn. (See Equine Studies at the back of the book.)

Visit your local tack shop—or preferably more than one—and ask more than one associate which lesson facilities he or she would recommend and why.

Finally, pay a visit to those you have decided might be good, reputable riding centers, dedicated to teaching you to ride—even if they are also dedicated to showing horses.

Some barns identify themselves as 'show barns,' which generally means they will be better for you after you've at least gotten to intermediate rider skills and have a nice horse you would like to show. Some, however, are equally adept at teaching beginners and like to do it, knowing that today's beginners are tomorrow's horse owners.

Straight from the horse's mouth

Watch a few lessons at the candidate barns. Here's what to look for:

Patience with students, especially beginners. (As noted earlier, some experienced instructors feel diminished by teaching beginners. However, those who understand the sport—and their own business!—will welcome them. Not only are they the future, if they are started right, they will be a joy to teach and to watch, rather than a frustrating re-training exercise.)

Absence of negative or denigrating instructions or comments to students; no matter what mistake a student makes, an instructor should **NEVER** berate a student.

Happy faces.

Respectful interaction between instructor and students.

Reasonable accommodation for parents to observe classes...but check, too, to see that parents are not allowed to interfere.

For adult beginner classes, check to see that the instructor does not talk down to the students.

Although it will be difficult, assess whether all or most of the students display improved skills between the beginning and end of the class; failing that, talk with them and see how they feel about what they are learning. Or, take a knowledgeable friend with you who can visually assess the progress in the classes.

Ask for barn tour, and observe well.

Are the aisles clean? Realize that clean in a barn isn't the same as clean in a house. There will be some dirt from recently picked hooves, and a few wisps of hay and so on. What you shouldn't see is a pile of trash in the aisle, more than one pile of 'road apples' in any horse's stall, wet and stinky stalls, dirty saddles and bridles laying around and so on.

Is hay stored away from chemicals and electrical equipment?

Do aisles show signs of having been swept that day?

Are fences in reasonably good repair? Horses will kick boards down overnight, so one missing board is not a bad sign; several would be.

Look into the lesson tack room.

Does each saddle have a rack, and each bridle a hook? Are they adequately labeled so a student can easily pick the tack for his or her horse?

Is there a bathroom for students, or at least a frequently cleaned portajohn? If there is only a portajohn, is there running water in the barn so that students can wash up?

Check that there is water in each horse's stall, maybe not a full bucket (they do tend to drink at will!) but none should be empty, and none should have a film on the top of the water, nor be full of sodden hay or otherwise indicate that the buckets are seldom scrubbed.

Down to business

If the lessons appear to be informative, fun, and safe, and the barns appear to be clean and horses well kept, the next stop is the office. In a large barn, there may be staff and even an office manager. In a small barn, you will probably find that the office, if any, is tiny and will be staffed when possible by the owner or head trainer (sometimes the same person) or barn manager.

Sometimes, in a very small barn, the owner is all three, although she or he may have day labor to help clean stalls and turn horses out and bring them in. In some cases, 'working students' trade labor for lessons, too.

Warning! If working students do give lessons, be sure they are well advanced and well supervised, or better still, are doing some 'fine-tuning' with individual students in a group lesson with the hired trainer also in the arena.

In the office, in most states, a lesson barn inspection document of some sort should be available, whether from the state agriculture department or other designated agency. Ask to see it. In some states, there are ratings for riding academies and lesson barns.

Ask to see the Liability Release the barn uses: if the barn has none, then it is flying under the radar and is probably uninsured and you just plain don't want to ride there.

The release will state that you realize that riding horses and/or dealing with horses is inherently dangerous, and beyond reasonable care by the barn of your safety and so on, you assume full responsibility for your safety. You will have to sign a release to ride there; if you are unwilling to sign one, then you are not ready to learn to ride. Riding IS inherently dangerous. Horses weigh about a thousand pounds and have hooves and teeth and a kick that makes Mike Tyson's right arm look like overcooked spaghetti. Accept those facts, and choose a barn that limits any possibility of danger as much as humanly possible, and you'll have a great time on horseback. Deny it, and 'cowboy' around and act like you're immortal, and you might find out just how mortal you really are.

Consider the program itself

If you are satisfied to this point, before you sign the release and sign up for lessons, there is one more indication of reputability and quality of teaching that you've got to run down: The way the lesson program is run.

Most medium to large barns will run semesters (often 10 to 12 weeks, with allowance for summer camp weeks when regular lesson programs are tough to run, what with all the kids on site all day), or will ask you to pay for a month up front. Both of these methods are reasonable, with exceptions. If you are allowed only one 'make-up' class during a semester, forfeiting any others you might need to miss, that barn might be more interested in its cash flow than in your learning to ride. Or worse, perhaps it cannot keep students any other way because the teaching is so bad. The first issue may not offend you, although I think it bespeaks a less-than-passionate horseperson. Do you really want such a person to be in charge of your well being?

The second issue is, however, crucial. Being allowed only one make-up class during a month is reasonable, by any standards. When these make-ups are scheduled, they should be at the discretion of the instructor to be sure your make-up lesson will be neither too far below nor too far above your current skill level. Being allowed only one make-up lesson in 12 to 14 weeks is not reasonable, considering the demands on parent/adult time these days, not to mention academic demands on young riders.

As for costs, private or semi-private lessons will be more expensive than group lessons. However, until you can reliably walk and trot and canter a little, they can be a good investment. The individual attention will get you into riding and give you a better understanding of the horse and how it operates—and your part in that—much quicker and more thoroughly than would happen in a group, especially if the group is five, six, seven or even eight.

Warning! No reputable barn interested in safety and learning will schedule one-hour group lessons with more than six regular students, allowing for one rider doing a make-up lesson, also, at the instructor's discretion. If there are more students in a group than seven— regardless of the gargantuan size of the arena— then there should be an assistant instructor also in the arena.

And, too, be sure the arena is big enough to handle six horses at once without having any of them in danger of running into jumps or each other before rider steering gets to a minimally competent level. How will you know this? Observe. Horses should be able to have a 'personal space' around them on all sides of at least four horse-lengths, although students may have a hard time actually keeping that distance. (They should be taught, over time.) But it should be possible. Some barns have huge arenas that can accommodate 20 horses with all maintaining adequate spacing.

If the barn regularly schedules hour-long group lessons with any more than 8 mounted students, run from there as fast and as far as you can. No instructor can possibly give good value to that many students—especially beginners—in a vast space where some may be out of earshot, making it doubly dangerous. If there is an assistant, and that assistant is knowledgeable and not just an older intermediate student lacking the years to lend authority to her voice in a pinch, use your discretion regarding value for money and safety.

Other factors to consider in the riding arena

When you are watching lessons, it is likely that people who own their own horses will want to ride, or hack, them. If they are allowed into the arena while lessons are going on, watch how that is done. If they are required to ask the instructor for permission to enter, you will know the barn is operating in a respectful manner at least, with lesson students given preference; after all, lesson students only have an hour of riding a week, generally, while owners can ride at will.

Once the owner and horse are in the arena, watch to see if they yield to the class and work in the same direction—very important!—that the class is working in. Why is this important? With beginning riders, especially, it is important to limit confusion and sensory input; the riders have an awful lot of information coming at them, and they are in an unfamiliar setting on a 'vehicle' they do not know how to operate.

Yet, it's a vehicle with a mind of its own; you don't want rude riders scaring the horses, either. It is essential for barns and instructors to do everything they can to ensure that beginners are not overfaced (given tasks that are beyond their skills at the moment), overmounted (given a horse that is too much horse for them to ride at the moment), or intimidated by those to whom horses have become routine. Putting beginner students in needlessly dangerous situations is inexcusable, and signifies a careless riding environment.

Avoid dangerous situations

Reputable barns try to limit possibilities for injury to riders or horses; careless barns do not. Observation will tell you which sort of barn you are looking at.

Needlessly dangerous situations include, but are not limited to:

Giving beginner lessons in an unenclosed space, such as an open field with no sturdy fence in sight.

Trash blowing around the arena.

Farm/barn implements left around the arena, including drags for grooming the arena.

Allowing children to run and climb on fences and tables/trees/whatever surrounding the riding arena.

Workers doing routine maintenance in the arena vicinity while lessons are in progress. This includes painting arena fences, replacing arena light bulbs in an indoor arena (or outdoor, for that matter, if it is an all-weather/24-hour arena), moving tottery bales of hay with a noisy front-loader, and so on.

Beginners are having a hard enough time making the transition from being a normal person to being a 'horseperson.' Allowing needless environmental stresses to occur at a time when they should be concentrating on developing basic skills and having some fun is not a sign of a properly run program.

A matter of money

Finally, you need to know what the lessons will cost and how they are to be paid for. Virtually all programs will want payment for the month ahead, or even the semester ahead.

If you must sign up for the semester, be sure there is an opportunity for some sort of refund if, after two or three lessons of the 12 or so you decide riding is not for you.

If you take private lessons, they are generally paid for when you take the lesson rather than ahead of time.

Do not automatically equate "most expensive" with "best." Lessons that are expensive compared to others in the area might not necessarily be the best, or the best for you. You may thrive in an expensive show barn with a great trainer, or you may thrive in a small boarding barn where an experienced horsewoman takes on only a few students, charging very little, but giving them everything she knows. So, in addition to assessing the safety, teaching ability and lesson program design, you'll need to assess the sort of experience you are looking for: Busy and targeted, or laid back and accommodating.

Decide how much you are willing to pay. It is reasonable to adjust lesson frequency to afford better instructors. **NEVER** overbook yourself in cheap, but inferior, lessons just for "saddle time," as valuable as saddle time is to learning to ride. It must be good saddle time; bad saddle time is worse than none, and you'd be better off watching tapes of excellent riders and at least intellectually learning from them. In the end, cheap, bad lessons may keep you from every becoming an accomplished rider, no matter how often your seat has been in the saddle's seat.

At a very small barn, you may have to agree to take a particular group lesson or private lesson time, but you are unlikely to have to pay for it ahead of time; these barns generally work on a pay-as-you-go basis, which works well for adults' busy schedules. But of course, they do ask a commitment, since they will be holding that spot for you, and would like a call as far ahead as possible if you cannot make it on any given day.

When you are satisfied that you have found the best mix of teacher, barn and cost for yourself or your child—for anyone else—sign up.

What to expect in lessons

You will probably be sore after your first lesson; the muscles used to ride are a whole different combination than you will have used for any other sport. So that's normal.

You should be exhilarated because, for the first time, you will have been able to ask a horse to walk, direct its movements, and stop it again.

You should not be frightened (beyond the excited kind of fear) or demoralized. If you are, you must assess whether it is because the instructor was careless or ignored you or your concerns, or whether you are simply over-reacting for reasons of your own. Perfectionism. Timidity. Stress. Something else. Realize that you will not do everything right at first, and don't allow correction by the instructor to upset you. Get upset, instead, if you are not corrected! Actually, even after you are an accomplished rider, after some rides, you will feel unsatisfied with your progress; after others, you may burst at the seams with feelings of your own perfection.

Warning! Your instructor should never, no matter what mistakes you might make, berate or belittle you. If an instructor contributes in any way to feelings of worthlessness, find a different place to ride.

If you have decided to train yourself, at least in part, and have purchased a horse to do so, be aware that you will not always succeed in what you set out to do on horseback, and give yourself a break. If it were easy to ride horses, if there was never any fear involved, the whole world would ride them. And even pre-automobile, not everyone could ride. Or wanted to.

Remember this: Whether you choose a lesson program, private lessons at a barn, or private lessons on your own horse at home, you have decided that riding will be fun, and it's a skill you want to master. That puts you into a rare group, no more than one tenth of one percent of the world's population.

You don't ride perfectly? So what? It's a miracle that humans can ride the huge elemental beasts♥ at all, and there you are, doing it. Congratulations!

♥ Author Dick Francis, former steeplechase jockey for H.R.H. Queen Elizabeth, refers to horses by that term in his best-selling mystery novels about British steeplechase racing. Francis gives readers a good feel for what being passionate about horses and riding is all about, and is a good read for horse fans.

Chapter Seven: Basic Equipment for Safe Riding

Cowboys wear jeans and pointy-toed boots with a relatively high heel for a reason. The jeans protect their legs from the hard leather of a western saddle and from the bushes and brambles and tumbleweed they might encounter out on a ride. The boot heels help keep their feet properly placed in the wide, leather-covered western stirrups. The pointy toes? I'm clueless. Ask a western rider.

Most people have jeans in their closet; many have western boots purchased as fashion items. No one questions this riding attire.

But many question why English/hunt seat riders wear tall boots and breeches, or short boots and jodhpurs. And some beginners at hunt seat erroneously think that they can wear anything rough and ready—cowboy wear, for example—and learn to ride.

Perhaps they can. But there is a lot to be said for looking the part; actors use costume to help them become their role. Just so, riders who look like riders, in the style of riding they are learning, assume the role of rider much more easily.

And, while I don't advocate using equipment as a substitute for good skills, improper equipment can keep you from getting those skills as easily and quickly as you otherwise might. If you are fighting the pain caused by tough jeans' welted seams, you may be reluctant to use your body as you should in an English saddle. If your feet are always slipping out of the irons because the narrow, curved, pointy sole of your western boot makes it so, you will not only have a harder time learning the proper and effective English leg position, you will be in greater danger.

It is true that a fully experienced rider should be able to hop on an English-trained horse bareback wearing shorts and sneakers—and a helmet!—and get the job done. And they can. But they had proper equipment to get to that place of consummate skill and knowledge and balance.

So, as they might have said in 1890, let's hear no more whining about the necessity of acquiring the proper equipment.

Look over the two lists below, the first for junior riders (those under age 12) and the second for adults, and plan to acquire these essential items the very minute you know you are dedicated to becoming a rider:

Proper equipment for junior riders

- Approved helmet
- Jodhpurs (also called jods)
- Paddock boots
- Cotton pimple-palm gloves (summer), knitted wool pimple-palm gloves or thin leather gloves (plain or Thinsulate®-lined) for winter
- Acceptable winter outerwear
- Acceptable warm weather tops
- For girls with long hair: scrunchies

Proper equipment for adult riders

- Approved helmet
- Jodhpurs
- Paddock boots
- Cotton pimple-palm gloves (summer), knitted wool pimple-palm gloves or thin leather gloves (plain or Thinsulate®-line) for winter
- Acceptable winter outerwear
- Acceptable warm weather tops
- For women with long hair: scrunchies

Does this look awfully similar to the juniors list? It is, and it should be. For adults, there are just a couple of additions and changes that will be noted where appropriate.

The equipment, explained

For Children

Approved helmets: Your first question might be "Approved by whom?" By the Safety Equipment Institute which developed from the American Society for Testing and Materials. The helmet should specify that it is ASTM/SEI approved. If it is not, don't buy it.

The United States Centers for Disease Control offers information developed for the National Ag Safety Database that will help you understand the importance of approved helmets. "Bicycle helmets reduce traumatic brain injuries in bicyclists by 88 percent.20. The effectiveness of ASTM/SEI equestrian helmets is estimated to be comparable," the CDC notes. They advise, "Consistent use of secured, ASTM-standard, SEI-certified equestrian helmets will lead to a decrease in equestrian deaths and serious injuries." ♥

In the old days, helmets were not worn for jumping, and not even for English riding except non-protective hunt caps as part of the costume for those who rode to hounds.

When jumping began to be a major spectator sport, top-level riders wore hunt caps, those same black velvet, close-fitting caps with a visor in front and flat bow at the back worn by British foxhunters. Those early caps, however, offered minimal protection. They were usually lined with a single layer of hard plastic (if anything at all

---

♥ The reference material may be accessed at
http://www.cdc.gov/nasd/docs/d000901-d001000/d000978/2.html.

beyond the stiff card needed to produce the shape), and they had no chinstrap. Most often, they were no longer on the rider's head when he or she hit the ground during a spill.

Fortunately, by the 1980s, hunt caps were being made with at least some padding inside and often chin straps attached, as well. Professionals still tended to wear the virtually non-protective kind. And in truth, the minimal padding in those helmets only helped in a minimal fall. The rider still risked serious injury in a serious fall.

By the late 1980s, people were beginning to realize two things: Riding hunt seat and jumping are serious sports, and loads more people than ever before were beginning to participate. Those two factors opened the way for a greater number of potential head injuries.

At the time, bicycle riders were already using protective headgear, and they were on a vehicle that is, first, much smaller than a horse and, second, does not have a mind of its own.

The issue was settled: It was high time to improve helmets and set some standards. Those early helmets were ugly, though. And some advanced amateurs during those years—myself included—refused to buy them, preferring the less bulky minimally protective old style helmet.

AHA! Did I say helmet? About that time, it became acceptable to call them helmets or hunt cap or hat interchangeably, signaling that finally, the hunter-jumper world had decided protection was a good thing.

These days, if a rider says, "Would you hand me my hat?" they almost invariably mean their helmet, shaped like the old-style hunt cap but offering infinitely more protection. And thankfully, the current generation of helmets has been manufactured with much better technology. So, even though they have linings of expanded polystyrene, which crushes on impact so that your head won't, they are less bulky and are really, finally, altogether acceptable in every way. Even today's professionals—myself included—would not even sit on a horse without a modern, approved ASTM/SEI helmet in place.

A proper fit, though, is just as important as a proper helmet. The helmet should fit snugly around the cranium, and the front edge of the brim (the inside brim, not the visor) should lie right above the brow ridge. *Right above it.* The helmet should not be tipped back so that the visor points toward the sky. The visor should extend straight out, perpendicular to the forehead.

To check the fit, flatten your hands and place one on each side of the helmet and try to rock it. It should take a small amount of pressure, about the same as a firm handshake, to get it to rock a little. If the person being fitted says it also feels OK—not too tight—then adjust the chinstrap so it is firmly under the chin, not choking the rider, but with virtually no 'wiggle room' either. Then have the rider jump, spin, or make some dance movements. If the helmet doesn't wobble, it's probably a pretty good fit.

Do not, however, depend on the fit to keep it on the head; make sure the chin strap is also in place, fastened, and tight enough to prevent centrifugal force from separating the hat even half an inch from contact with the head in the case of accident. The design of the helmet is such that it protects the brain best when it remains seated with the back coming well down to cover the place where the spinal column enters the skull.

To fit the chin strap, you may have to adjust two straps, one that attached toward the rear of the helmet and one that attaches at the sides; these meet in a single strap on each side that can also be adjusted. Adjustments should balance the helmet so that, if bumped, it does not migrate forward or backward. It does take a few minutes, but need only be done once and checked occasionally to see that the adjustments have not altered through use and wear.

Warning! *Do not buy a used helmet.* You cannot know whether the helmet has been through an accident. If it has, it may have cracks beneath the fabric you cannot see. And even if you could look beneath the fabric cover, you couldn't tell if there were weaknesses only technology could identify.

(Feel free, though, to save a little money buying used clothing and boots when you can. Old horsepeople know, too, that buying a slightly used saddle is often a great deal; someone else went through the painful process of breaking it in—suppling the leather through use and applications of leather dressing.)

Hunt caps/helmets come in several varieties. There is the traditional velvet or velveteen-covered cap, and that's what's needed, adult or junior, for showing a horse. But they are very hot in summer, especially compared to the vented colorful plastic helmets now available. You can choose a plastic helmet and vary the look (kids love this!) with fancy nylon covers in wild patterns, or sporty ones (cross-country riders like the two-color type in sporty colors, such as burgundy and blue and so on). And you can get a black velveteen cover for showing, making the one helmet do the job of two, often a wise idea as children do outgrow their first helmet, and maybe even their second.

Different manufacturers' products also suit different head shapes. Some are elongated, some more round. One manufacturers' hats will fit you, in general, better than those of others. Once you've found out which, replacing helmets will not be nearly as difficult, and you can probably do it via mail order. But for the first helmet, go to a good tack shop and get fitted. Then you'll know your size, and which manufacturer's styles suit your head.

Jodhpurs: Why not jeans? Because in English equitation, you ride so close to the saddle that the seams in jeans leave welts and cause pain once the child is past the very beginning stages of riding. "Jods" are made of fabric that's easily washed and quickly dried, meaning there's no need for more than a pair or two. Juniors can wear jodhpurs with paddock (low) boots to show horses, too, although adults need breeches with tall boots.

Jodhpurs should be long enough to come down to the ankle or even a little below. Jods will be held in place while riding by elastic bands that run from one side of the pants leg to the other, under the sole of the boot. (These are purchased separately) Buy jodhpurs that have suede or suede-like knee patches rather than patches of the same stretch fabric as the jods. This will help keep the rider's leg in the proper place, difficult to do at first in a slick, smooth English saddle.

Jods come in beige, a light neutral greenish-beige, rust, pearl gray and often black or navy blue. The child will need beige, greenish-beige or pearl gray for showing, so if you can buy only one pair, buy one of those colors. If you can buy more, then also consider a dark color for variety. Or you can even consider plaid, or the many 'fashion update' patterns that appear in the equine clothing catalogs from time to time. **Hint:** Because arena dust is some version of sand-colored, the light-colored breeches show dirt less than the darker ones do. But a heavy child might like the slimming effect of the darker color until he or she loses weight—which riding will help with.

You can also get schooling tights, sometimes with wild stripes down the side of the leg, and those, too, are appropriate if the school allows them for lessons, as long as they have the proper, 'grippy' knee patches.

Riding itself will help any child's self-esteem; making sure they look as good as possible while learning will help, too. The same applies to adults.

Paddock boots: These are boots that lace up above the ankle. They often have steel, or at least hardened, toes. And the heel height is the proper one for riding English. Many young riders start riding wearing hiking boots or some sort of fashion boot, but that is really not acceptable after the first one or two lessons and the student is beginning to learn to post the trot. Aside from the fact that the soles are not designed for use in stirrups, and may cause the foot to slip out or through (either of which is bad, with 'through' being worse), they usually offer no ankle support, nor will they prevent stirrup leathers from gouging tender ankle skin as the rider gets stronger and puts more 'leg' against the horse.

Most barns frown on sneakers/running shoes of any sort, as they should. (Some prohibit their use outright.) This is for the same reason hiking or other non-riding boots are frowned upon after the initial lesson or two. With sneakers, the foot can slide through the stirrup iron, which could be painful, or even dangerous if the horse acted up. Like hiking boots, they fail to protect the lower leg from the rubbing of stirrup leathers. And worse— worse even than hiking boots—they offer no protection if a horse misplaces a foot while you're working on the ground, and steps on your toes.

During the lesson itself, because sneakers are so soft, a placid school horse may not even recognize it as a request to move when a junior rider applies them to his sides, making the rider's job much harder than it needs to be. If the training is good, the rider—junior or adult—will be taught to ask the horse to move with the legs, but the feet enter into it at first, until the rider learns that a horse will respond to a press and not a kick. The hard leather uppers and hard sole of a real paddock boot is something the horse can easily feel and respond to, keeping beginner frustration at a lower level.

Paddock boots come in two styles, lace-up and zip-up. The zip-up style is also known as a jockey boot, and not a good choice for a junior rider for several reasons. First, they are not proper for showing. Second, they have elastic gussets on the sides, making it hard to get a snug—not tight, just snug—fit at the top to protect the ankle and offer support. Another problem is that, when one has to walk into a muddy paddock to bring in a horse—and beginners are taught to do this at most barns—the mud makes the zippers stick and wear out.

When you buy the boots, buy a leather conditioner, as well. Before the first wearing, rub it all over the boot, with extra at the ankle area. Also rub some INSIDE the boot at the ankle area. Although the boots need to fit snugly and stay tied, they also have to be quite flexible at the ankle because English riding requires a foot position in which the toe is higher than the heel, and while the boots should support and protect, they should not restrain.

Informed opinion: My personal favorite conditioner is Horseman's One-Step®; it both cleans the leather and conditions it in one application, and it's inexpensive. (You'll pay six or seven dollars for a tub that will last until the rider begins jumping, very likely.)

Many people prefer Lexol®-type products that are credited with keeping the leather in good condition for years. When you're new to the sport, though, getting some comfort quickly is a good thing; save the upscale, fancy dressings for your next pair of boots. Who knows? Maybe you'll buy custom boots that cost as much as a good used car and you'll want them to last 25 years. And they can, with some high-end leather dressing and good care...after you have first softened them with some One-Step®.

Gloves: It is good to ride sometimes without gloves because it is easier to develop a feel for the horse that way. But junior riders, particularly, sometimes have such tender hands that every time the horse moves his head, it causes friction on the reins that hurts the little hands. And in winter, of course, gloves are necessary even in temperate zones for all riders.

In horse shows, while gloves are not required, they are expected and when a judge must make a close decision, the rider who is better dressed, right down to the gloves, will probably get the ribbon. (In hunter, hunter-jumper and jumper competition, the winning rider/horse gets a blue ribbon, the second-place a red ribbon, and down through several more colors, usually to sixth place, although some very large shows 'pin' eight or even ten places. In the English riding world, winning is called "pinning.")

Winter outerwear: Contrary to popular belief, riding is a sport and a physically demanding one at that. If a rider is on a lazy horse, it's sort of like being on a nautilus machine that works the entire body for an hour. Riders can work up a sweat, even in frigid weather. So, when buying outerwear (and indeed underwear) for winter in temperate zones, buy layers. Silk long-john pants and silk t-shirts are great for really cold weather and are less bulky than regular thermals, although those will do. Silk glove liners are also handy. A heavy sweatshirt is a must-have. Many barns have logo shirts made up, and those are nice to have; kids especially like wearing them when they're not riding, so others know they do ride.

A down vest is another good investment; often a jacket is not needed, but, especially at the beginning of the ride, the torso often wants a little more weatherproofing than silk undies and a sweatshirt. Vests are easy to shed in that weather between seasons, or when one gets overheated while riding. They are also easy to wear under a short jacket (which should end at or just below the waist; it should not come down under the buttocks as that would interfere with position and safety. Barns often have logo jackets made up, also, which riders can buy. Often, those jackets have great zippered pockets to keep a few tissues in, or a couple of bite-size wrapped chocolates for quick energy, or, for adults, the car keys.)

Finally, there are the rider's exposed ears to consider; helmets do not come down over the ears, so what can you do? Tack shops sell ear protectors that either fit onto the straps of the helmet, or sit on the head in such a way that they do not interfere with the fit of the helmet. In a pinch, a knitted all-purpose ear protector/headband will do. Just be sure it doesn't force the helmet out of position.

Warm weather tops: No bandeau tops, no tiny little t-shirts, no fluffy tops, no tops with rattling things. The first two would cause serious 'road rash' on tender parts should the rider happen to fall off; the second two might spook a horse and *cause* a rider to fall off.

Proper summer tops include: regular t-shirts, polo shirts with short sleeves, ironed shirts with short sleeves and sleeveless polo shirts (NOT sleeveless t-shirts, or 'muscle' shirts.) Tank tops are sometimes acceptable in really hot climates, as long as they are not too low-cut, have low-cut armholes or too-skinny straps.

Save the tanks and sleeveless polos for really, really hot weather. And never wear them, even when schooling— that is, practicing—at a horse show. (Some barns will not permit tank tops at any time for any reason, so inquire before you buy or wear them for lessons.) The aim in riding English is not only to ride well and safely, but also to look as if you do, and that means dressing conservatively. A plain polo shirt is preferred, for example, to a loud t-shirt. But for lessons in most barns, either will do. When a child begins showing, he or she will need a proper buttoned shirt and jacket anyway.

Scrunchies: I know a trainer who won't let anyone who looks like Lady Godiva—who enters the ring with long, flowing hair—ride until she puts the hair up in a hairnet under her helmet, or secures it with a scrunchie. Part of the reason is the look. (Remember, if you look like a rider, you're more likely to act like a rider. And the more you 'act as if,' the quicker you're going to become what you desire to be.) But it is also safety; it can be a major interference to have wisps of hair stinging you in the eyes, or to have to reach up and take a strand or two out of your mouth. And there's this: to horses, blonde hair often looks like hay, and they sometimes actually try to nibble it!

So secure long hair in a scrunchie, just below the bottom edge of the back of the helmet. Or, French braid the hair; that usually lies flat enough not to interfere with the fit of the helmet, and the bow at the bottom looks nice, too. Most female junior riders with long hair wear it in two braids for the first few shows, with nice bows lying flat against the back of their jacket. As they get older, they sometimes put it into a net caught with a bow just below the back edge of the helmet, and that, too, looks very elegant and neat. (Adult female riders with all but the shortest hair must put their hair up into a hair net and tuck it all into the helmet when they show a hunter-jumper.)

For adults

While juniors can show in paddock boots and jodhpurs, adults must show in tall boots and breeches, although they can train in jods and paddock boots.

In addition to the schooling (that is, lesson) glove styles for junior riders, there are some other styles adults might consider, notably the gloves with leather palms and string backs. These are very useful for late winter/early spring and late fall/early winter in temperate climates. Plus, they are quite popular for field hunting, if that's the way you want to go eventually.

Field hunting is a term used almost interchangeably with fox hunting. A suitable horse for "riding to hounds' is a field hunter; the most usual difference between these horses and show hunter is in refinement. Field hunters are often bigger, bolder and more steady than their show-hunter counterparts. Those who prefer field hunting often prefer a good, long gallop to the more controlled technical ride used to get horses over pre-determined numbers of fences in a relatively small space, the arena. Both forms of English riding are popular, and many riders to both. Sometimes, the same horse can be used for both, as long as the horse is 'fancy' enough for the show ring (that is, has good conformation and way of going, or movement) and sturdy enough for fields and streams and rock walls.

As mentioned above, adult women with medium or long hair MUST put it up in a hairnet under the helmet when they are in horse show. But for lessons and hacking (just riding, in English parlance), securing it with a scrunchie or putting it in a French braid is just fine.

And then there are the boots. As you begin, you will probably ride in jods and paddock boots. That's fine.

Many riders invest in chaps to protect their legs from being burned by the stirrup leathers. Chaps also give a bit more sticking power, because of the leather-to-leather aspect. Be aware, though, that it is well to ride in jods and paddock boots sometimes, or breeches and tall boots, so you won't become dependent on the greater sticking power afforded by chaps.

Chaps can be a fashion statement, too. But they are also often a source of unfortunate one-upsmanship, something that does exist in equine sports, despite the insistence on sportsmanship regarding showing and riding itself.

Eventually, especially if you want to show someday or ride with a hunt, you'll need to get used to tall boots. Many riders, once they've experienced a ride in tall boots, never ride any other way again, except maybe the odd bareback ride in sneakers in the summer. Tall boots help the leg position stabilize, and they protect the leg from leather burns as the rider gains strength and a better position.

Tall boots come in two styles, field boots and dress boots. Of the two, most hunt seat riders prefer field boots. They are easier to get on than dress boots, for one thing, because the lacing right above the instep can be undone to allow a foot with a higher arch to enter the slender boots more easily. And there's that 'look' thing. Over the years, it has become traditional that hunt seat riders wear field boots, except when they move on to Open Jumpers, which means 5-foot fences...so that will take a while. And dressage riders wear dress boots although, at the lower levels of dressage, field boots are acceptable. So there it is: For the next several years of your riding, at the very least, a pair of field boots is your better choice. (Fashion hint: They also make long feet look smaller!)

Color considerations

The United States Equestrian Federation rulebook says that for shows, boots can be brown or black. In the past 20 years, I have seen exactly ONE pair of brown field boots in an arena at a show in the hunter ring. You can scarcely find them, except in custom-made boots. As a beginner, don't invest in custom boots. They cost $700, minimum. While they will last 20 years, your leg and foot may change as you gain more muscle tone. And you may want a different toe style and whatnot as you go on. So get off-the-rack tall boots. And get black. Move up to custom footwear when you really understand yourself as a rider.

Off-the-rack tall boots have both a foot size and a calf size. Go to the tack shop for your first pair, rather than ordering by mail, so you can be measured and taught how to properly put the boots on. (Putting them on requires boot pulls, which you will buy at the same time as the boots.) Getting them off requires either a very willing, very strong person who doesn't mind grabbing the filthy bottom of your boots—after all, they may have MUCK on them—or a bootjack. Buy the bootjack.)

Also buy some Horseman's One-Step® and a bunch of big, puffy Band-Aids. Properly fitted off-the-rack tall boots will hurt like mad until they are broken in (just live with it!) But you can help the breaking in period a lot by slathering One-Step inside and out especially at the ankle, where the stiff new boots will eventually fold, and along the top back edge, inside and out. The boots will bite into the tender part of your leg above the knee at first. So apply those Band-Aids® where they hit until they soften up and drop, which they will. Apply the One-Step and set the boots in the sun. Then, while they're softened up, put them on and wear them around the house for a while. Do this a few times before you ride in them. And tell your instructor you've got new boots on so he or she will go easy on you as it is a slightly different feel than 'bare' legs if you've ridden in paddocks and jods for a while.

Eyeglasses and contacts

It should go without saying that you want safety glass in your eyeglasses—or even non-prescription sunglasses—for riding. Some people like to use contact lenses for riding in the winter, as glasses can fog up from the heat generated by a hard-working rider in cold air.

Your eyes are important because where your eyes are looking is where your horse is going to go. Your own body language will follow your eyes, and your body's position will affect the horse. In addition, the direction of your eyes will influence the direction of your head, and its position. Your head weighs about 20 pounds, which is enough to influence the horse, as well. He can feel it if you are looking down, up, ahead, or to one side, and—to a point—he will automatically try to go in the direction of your gaze. To a point.

But every little bit helps. So do what you have to do to make sure your eyewear is comfortable for you and appropriate and lets you see what you need to see.

Other useful equipment to have

Crops and whips: Most beginners just hate the idea of striking a horse with a crop or bat or whip. (These are somewhat interchangeable terms, although each does actually mean a specific instrument.) And most beginners cannot yet handle all the operations they are expected to perform on horseback, never mind adding holding and using one of these aids. (Aids is a term used to describe what we use to influence a horse. The legs, hands and seat are natural aids. Whips, crops, bats and spurs are artificial aids.)

But it would be as well to acquire one of these now, so that you will have it when your instructor decides you need it. Tell your instructor you have one, but do not carry it into the lesson unless asked.

Just FYI, here are the descriptions of bats, crops and whips:

A bat is a long stick, often wrapped in a colorful binding, with a rubberized grip handle and a one-inch wide doubled leather popper, the popper being the end that strikes the horse. A jumping bat is the longest variety, and one you are unlikely to need until you are jumping very big fences, or encounter a very stubborn horse. A regular bat is somewhat shorter. A pony club bat, the shortest, is appropriate for young junior riders on ponies. Bats do not have wrist straps.

A crop is a long stick, also covered, and also having a slender handle. A crop is often topped with a button to keep it from slipping through the hands. The popper is doubled leather, but only about ¼ of an inch wide. There is usually a wrist strap because this is the aid traditionally used by foxhunters. If it slipped out of their hands, it wouldn't fall to the ground, saving them a dismount and remount to retrieve it, and the problems of catching up with the rest of the hunt.

In lesson work, it is best not to use the wrist strap, but just let it hang to make switching the crop from hand to hand easier; the crop is often switched to influence a particular side of the horse until the rider gains strength and skill. Plus, if it drops in the riding arena, it is no problem for the instructor to pick it up or the rider to dismount to retrieve it. (Although some instructors charge students 25 cents each time they drop a bat and need it retrieved, partly for fun and partly to influence the student to practice switching crops and reins properly.

A whip is a long, covered stick with a handle that has a string popper, rather than leather, on the end. Some horses respond better to this than to the leather popper.

Spurs: You won't need spurs until after you begin to canter and jump and your leg position is stable, in all likelihood. On the other hand, there are some very old, very lazy school horses that not only tolerate the imprecise use of a short spur by a beginner, but actually require the use of spurs to move at all. So invest in spurs; they won't spoil, and you never know when your instructor will call for them.

When you buy your first spurs, buy Tom Thumb spurs (the shortest shank, or part that touches the horse's side) or Prince of Wales (the next longest). Do not buy rowel spurs, ones with a moving wheel either with notches or without. These are sold in English tack shops, but they are for dressage use only and are not allowed in hunter shows. Some people use them to train hunters. But beginners will have no need of them; they are very harsh and take a very experienced, stable and tactful rider to use without abusing the horse.

Fly Spray: In almost any climate, this is handy to have in the summer. It doesn't matter what kind you buy; most are about equally effective. If you're so inclined, there are new all-natural fly sprays on the market, which is appealing since you will get the stuff on your hands and clothing. It's hard to imagine a thousand-pound horse being harmed by a little bit even of the older, more toxic sprays.

Use fly spray all over the horse—legs, body, neck and tail—but not his face, unless you spray it into your hand and rub it on his ears and face, but not too close to eyes, nostrils and lips.

You can also invest in a fly repellent roll-on for the horse's face, still being careful not to get it too close to his eyes, lips or nostrils.

Basic grooming kit: Some barns do not allow students to use their own grooming equipment because of the risk of carrying an infectious disease in from another barn where the student might take some lessons. But if the barn does allow personal grooming kits, or you have bought a horse and either board it or keep it at home, a grooming kit is essential.

You can purchase pre-fitted grooming kits, with all you will need to get started. Or you can put together your own box. You will need a plastic box with a handle, available in both tack shops and stores that carry household cleaning items. And you will need the equipment listed below.

Minimal grooming equipment includes:
Currycomb
Hard brush
Medium brush
Soft brush
Rub rag
Hoof pick
Comb

You will also want to buy a plastic tote to carry them in. Remember to clean the tote out occasionally because it will collect hair and dirt. And remember to wash the contents of the kit as well.

To clean brush, use warm, soapy water. Rinse them well, and set them outside, preferably on some grass in the sun, to dry. Dry off the wooden handles and then set them down bristle-side down so the water drains out and does not warp the wood.

Chapter Eight: Getting Ready to Ride

Before you ride, you will have to groom your horse and tack him up. Even if you plan to ride bareback, there are two things you must *always* do for your horse before you ride:

1. Pick the dirt and stones out of his hoof.

2. Brush off all dirt where the bridle will go and where the saddle will go, or, if riding bareback, where you will sit.

If it is summer, you will also want to fly spray the horse, both for his comfort and yours. Learning to ride on a horse that's fidgeting because of flies just makes it that much harder to learn and have fun. Take the bottle of spray with you to the arena or the field and apply more as sweat and dust dilutes the spray's effectiveness.

Most often, you will need to give your horse a full grooming. If you are riding school horses at a lesson barn, they will probably insist on a full grooming before and after each ride. If you own your horse, you'll want to take care of your investment, for his health and your continued enjoyment.

Note: A full grooming gets the horse clean, arguably warms up his muscles a bit, and cleans debris out of his feet. Grooming is considered to goof for horses than an old horseman's saying holds that, "A grooming is as good as a feed" for keeping horses healthy and happy.

Daily grooming

This is not the same as a show grooming. Show grooming is much more involved, and should leave the horse shining, hoofs pearly, mane either braided or, in today's less formal show atmosphere, properly pulled and combed. Lesson barns may teach you how to do this at some point, but for lessons, serviceably clean will do.

How to groom a horse

Put a halter on the horse. If the barn offers them, attach him to crossties, ropes with snap ends hooked to each side of an aisle wall. Apply the snaps to the metal rings on the halter that are placed either side of the horse's muzzle, NOT the ones up near his eyes/crown of head. This is for the safety of the horse.

If there are no cross-ties but rather tie rings fastened to the wall, use the loose ring under the horse's chin to attach the snap, then tie the lead rope to the tie ring with a quick-release knot.

How to tie a quick–release knot

Using the tie ring, position your horse close to the wall so that you can have the maximum length of lead rope available for tying the knot. Run two or three feet of rope through the ring. Hold both pieces of rope as they hang from the ring in one hand. Fold the rope's tail end (the free end, not the one attached to the horse), cross that piece over the two pieces in your hand and then through the loop that results. Pull the loopy end (called the bight) through the loop. Pull until the knot is secure and then slide it up toward the tie ring.

To undo this knot, all you need to do is tug on the loose end, and the knot will fall away, releasing the horse.

Warning! When tying the knot, keep your fingers out of the inside of loops so that, if your horse pulls away suddenly for any reason, you will not be hurt. You can catch a loose horse; broken fingers would probably be somewhat more problematical to deal with.

Why a quick-release knot in the first place?

So the horse will not pull the wall apart if he is really frightened of something and insistent on getting away. Or, in the case of a tornado approaching—for an extreme example—so you can set him free quickly to do what horses have always done—outrun it, and you can head for an inside stall, the bathroom or a root cellar...some kind of human cover, anyway.

When you have secured your horse, begin grooming. Keep one hand always on the horse so that he will know where your body is in relation to his. Horses have odd vision, so don't assume that where you can see, he can see, especially right in front of his face. On the other hand, most horses can see behind themselves much better than humans can, so that any sudden movement from behind might cause the horse to make a sudden move away from it. Keeping contact with him lets him know where you are, and, arguably, that there is nothing to fear. (Did I mention that, for all their size and speed, most horses are quite timid?)

Begin with the currycomb, an oval-shaped hard rubber item. Put your dominant hand through the strap and begin stroking it hard over the horse's coat in a circular motion against the direction of hair growth. Do this all over the body, beginning at the top of the neck and working toward the tail. Do not curry the head and legs below the knees.

Currying scrapes up the embedded dirt, which you will next brush off with the hard brush. Use this in straight strokes in the same direction as hair growth all over the body except the head and lower legs, again, working from head to tail.

Move on to the medium brush. With the tougher types of horses or if you have really bad embedded dirt, use this on the lower legs, but not—if you can help it—on the face. If you must get crusty dirt off the face, be sure to protect the horse's eyes with a cupped hand as you work with the softest brush that will do the job.

(Some instructors object to ever using this or a hard brush on a horse's lower leg. They believe it will hurt the tendons. Perhaps, if you are a weightlifter and do it with all your strength twice a day, every day. The occasional bruising with a medium or even a hard brush will not harm the horse, and sometimes it is necessary to remove caked on mud, which would harm the horse by setting up tender tissue for fungus to enter.)

Next, use the soft brush all over the body, even on the face. Use your hand to shield the horse's eyes as you work on the face. You might add to your equipment a very small brush—a face brush—which many horses like quite a bit.

Finish off with the rub rag to make the coat shine.

In seasons when there are a lot of flies, spray the horse all over with the fly spray after grooming; don't spray his head. For the head, you can either use a fly repellent roll-on or cream, or you can spray a little liquid fly spray into your hand and rub it on, avoiding the eyes and the nostrils. Rubbing it on the ears is a good idea. (Some horses are so sensitive to flies that their owners use fly nets over their ears in summer, even when they are being ridden.)

Next, comb the mane.

Do not comb out the tail unless the owner/instructor asks you to. Tails get very knotted, and unless you have lots of time to work with each knot, you can pull out so many hairs that the tail looks sparse and unattractive very quickly. Most horse owners comb out the tail only occasionally and/or before shows.

Finally, pick the hoofs. This is usually frightening to beginners who are also surprised by the amount of strength it requires.

How to pick a hoof

The hoof consists of a hard part, which is basically white under whatever dirt may have accrued (except in black-hoofed horses, in which case it is black).

About hooves: Some horses have both black and white material in the exterior hoof wall. Usually, this occurs in dark horses that have socks or stockings. Most farriers consider white hoof material to be much weaker than black; they believe hoofs with some black stripes are slightly to very much stronger.

Beginning at the heel of each foot is a triangular area of soft tissue called the frog. Do not scrape or pick this area with the hoof-picking tool. The frog acts as cushion for the delicate bones within the foot. It is sensitive and would be injured by a hoof pick. Rather, scrape the hard part that feels like a very big, very hard fingernail. And, if you must remove dirt from the frog, use a brush.

To get out the dirt, you'll have to pick up each of the horse's feet. Here's how:

Front feet: To pick up a front foot, stand directly next to the near (horse's left front leg) leg, as close as you can get, facing the horse's rear. Run your hand down the back of the leg. Just above the ankle, pinch the hollow between the tendons (this will be obvious) between thumb and forefinger, simultaneously pulling up. A trained horse should lift his foot off the ground. Even an untrained horse is likely to lift his foot if the pressure is strong enough.

Next, slide your left hand under the front of the hoof and use your strength to help hold the hoof in a cocked position in your hand so that, bending from the waist, you can clearly see the whole bottom of the foot.

Warning! Never kneel when working with a horse's feet. If you need to get down really low— for a pony, for example—bend from the waist or, as a last resort, squat. Do not kneel. If the horse got upset and walked toward you, you could not get out of his way fast enough from a kneeling position. From a bend or squat, you can remove yourself to safety in an instant.

Beginning at the rear of the hoof next to the frog, insert the point of the hoof pick into any dirt caught there, and flick it out. Continue around the hoof. Be aware that mud can require quite a bit of strength to break through and pull out. Then put the hoof down gently. (If the horse does not wear shoes, the hoofs must still be picked, although it is much, much easier. The metal shoe forms a rim that helps trap mud and debris in the hollow formed by the shoe.)

Go to the other front hoof and do the same thing. Stand next to his off (horse's right side) leg, facing rear and reversing the hand you use to pick and hold the hoof.

If your dominant hand is your right hand, picking the horse's near side front hoof will be easiest. If your dominant hand is your left, the left will be easier. Why? Because you will hold the hoof up with your non-dominant hand and pick with the dominant hand. Remember, you will be facing the horse's rear, so that, on his near (left) side, your left hand will be closer to him, and on the off side (right), your right hand will be closer.

Hind feet: Getting the rear hooves off the ground and into your hand is a bit trickier. Indeed, most beginners fear the hind feet; they fear being kicked. The fact is, horses often have a hard time maintaining the hind feet in a position off the ground long enough for the hoof to be picked, so the hoof might go up and down a little or to the side (really scary!) But school horses in general will stand for hoof picking.

The secret to safety while picking hoof is always to get really, really close to the horse. Then, if something upsets him and he does kick out a little, he cannot 'nail' you, but only push you aside. Plus, you will be touching him and know where his body is at all times, giving yourself a better chance to take evasive action or correct him if he does not stand like a perfect horse. And he will know where you are, which, as noted before, is important to him.

Facing the rear of the horse, stand just in front of the rear leg. Run one hand down the inside of the lower leg, looking for the groove as on the front legs. Squeeze it a little until the horse lifts his hoof, and then slide one hand under the exterior front hoof wall, just as with the front hoof.

Begin to pick the hoof, just as you did for the front feet. Be aware that some horses have a hard time with their hind feet. Some raise their foot very, very high, even letting the foot bob up and down a bit, which makes picking harder than for front hooves.

Other horses barely lift the hoof, depending on the groomer to lift the hoof high enough to see to pick; these horses are usually fond of resting the whole weight of their leg in the groomer's hand, too, making it a strain for small people working with large horses. There is not much help for it except practice and increasing strength. Young riders and petite adults, and anyone who is frightened by hoof-picking—especially the hind feet— should call for help from the instructor or barn manager until the rider is more confident around the hind feet.

You must respect a horse's hind feet, but you need not be afraid of them as long as you stand correctly, and monitor the horse's reactions to you and the environment so you can move out of range quickly if need be.

If you are learning to ride on your own, invest in some serious grooming and tacking up lessons, get an instructional tape, or go to work in a barn for free, as long as they agree to teach you various 'ground' things, such as grooming and stall mucking and bedding and so on.

How to tack up the horse

When the horse is clean, it's time to tack up.

Get the saddle, saddle pad, girth and bridle (with bit and reins attached, and properly fitted to the horse) and put them on racks in the aisle, if any. If there is no saddle rack, put the saddle down with the seat facing the wall, the front of the saddle (pommel) on the ground, and the cantle tipped up against the wall. This protects the tree, which makes the saddle's shape. If a tree gets broken, it may well injure the horse and will be fairly costly to repair. Find a hook or knob to hang the bridle on in the absence of a bridle hook or rack. Always hang it by the crown piece, with reins looped up over the hook as well.

Saddling

Put the saddle on first, while the horse is still cross-tied or tied to a tie ring.

Note, however, that there are two schools of thought on this.

Some believe one should bridle first, on the theory that, with the bit in place, you have more control of the horse. But this requires saddling with the reins looped over one arm. This is more 'input' than most beginners can handle, and I believe endangers them. It requires keeping an eye on the horse so you're not hurting him with the bit, keeping an eye on his feet so you don't get stepped on, walking completely around the horse with reins in tow. It is simply too much for a beginner. And, too, it violates the

Second Rule of Learning to Ride:

Above all else, sacrifice tack for safety.

Those who favor the bridle-first method think that it is more likely that a horse will bolt with the saddle on when you have him briefly 'free' while you take the halter off to put the bridle on, and they want to save their saddle.

When you're beginning to ride, I believe this is likely to get you and/or the horse in trouble. You might leave the reins looped over your arm way past the time you can actually dissuade a horse from bolting. You might annoy the horse greatly by tugging at his mouth with the bit as you make your way through the saddling maneuvers.

Leaving the reins dropped on the horse's neck is an invitation for him to leave and ruin ALL the tack. Horses are opportunists, as noted earlier, if nothing else.

Can a horse bolt with your saddle? Of course. But he can do that from a lead rope *or* a bridle. He's big. He's strong. You're not. So prepare to risk some saddle damage if your horse bolts. This will probably never happen with a trained school horse. But if it does, better damage to a saddle than to you.

Before putting on the saddle, you'll need to put the saddle pad on the horse. Saddle pads protect the horse's back from chafing; some have foam padding to protect horses with tender backs, especially when they must carry untrained, and therefore clumsy, riders.

If the pad is a contour pad, it will have the same shape as the saddle. It could also be a square pad, although usually hunt seat riders use a contour pad, while dressage riders prefer square. There are, of course, reasons for this. Hunt riders use the area right behind their leg to use a crop to influence a horse. Having fabric there would interfere. Dressage riders, on the other hand, use a long whip and generally touch their horse's flank with it, so there is no problem of fabric getting in the way.

You can tell the front of the contour pad easily; it is the straighter edge, without the extension for the back of the saddle. But what about a square pad? There will be straps to hold it in place under the saddle, and these will be in the front.

Fold the saddle pad in half. Lay the saddle pad across the horse's back with the front just at or in the center of the withers. Then place the saddle in the same place, making sure an edge of pad shows all around the saddle on both sides if a contour pad is used; you may have to adjust it. Do this by reaching under the pommel of the saddle and grasping the pad, pulling up on the excess until it goes some way into the channel, called the gullet, that runs down the middle of the saddle. Do this also with the square pad until some pad shows around the saddle all around. With a square pad, you won't want too much in front of the saddle, perhaps no more than ¾ of an inch. Allow more to show behind the saddle.

Pulling some saddle pad fabric up into the gullet ensures that the pad will not press uncomfortably into the horse's withers, which is, after all, part of his spinal column.

When the saddle is properly atop the pad, slide the saddle back just slightly so that the pommel of the saddle is at the withers.

Do attach the keepers by running one of the billet straps on the saddle to the pad on each side before buckling the girth to the billets. Why? Think of the saddle pad as equine underwear. You wouldn't like your underwear bunched up as you work or play, so why should the horse? Plus, a properly placed and fastened saddle paint protects sensitive skin from tough saddle leather.

Warning! Do not slide a saddle forward if you can help it. Rather, if you notice it has slid too far back, lift it, place it down again, and slide back again to the proper place. If you slide a saddle and pad forward, you will be going against the growth pattern of the horse's hair, making it catch in the fabric and causing discomfort, and even sores, for the horse.

Next attach the girth. Most girths have one end with elastic, one without. Facing the horse, begin on his right (off) side. Most of the time, you will see three billet straps under the flap of the saddle. There are only two buckles on the girth, though. Use the outer two billet straps, leaving the center one as a spare. This is so that, if one breaks when you are out on the hunt far from home, or at a show, you've got a spare and can still ride in safety with the saddle firmly attached.

> **Informed Opinion:** Some trainers prefer using two billets next to each other. I believe this allows for torque because it distributes the pull of the girth unevenly. In addition, beginners might use the back and middle billets on one side of the horse, the front and middle on the other, enhancing any tendency of the saddle to torque or slide under an unsteady beginner's seat and legs.

Attach the girth so that when it hangs down, it reaches to the horse's anklebone, give or take. Most often, this will allow you to attach it on the horse's left side (the near side) without struggle, and give you room to tighten it further before you ride. Before mounting, you should have the girth so tight that you can just barely put a single finger under it. Why? Because your entire weight will be pulling on it as you mount, and your weight in the saddle will squish it down and make it a bit looser and more comfortable for the horse as he goes.

Be sure the stirrup irons (in common rider parlance, simply irons) are at the top of the stirrup leathers against the stirrup bar, the metal piece that holds the stirrup leathers, before you walk the horse away from the grooming area. (Indeed, these must be up before you put the saddle on the horse.) Grasping the end of the doubled stirrup leather, use your other hand to slide the iron up the leather nearest the saddle. Then tuck the leather through the iron to hold it in place. Most irons will not slide back down the leather on their own, but you can also loop the loose end of the leathers around the footpad of the iron to further secure it while still allowing it to be brought down easily and quickly.

Bridling

To most beginners, this is the trickiest of all maneuvers, and offers the most possibility for letting a horse get loose. There is nothing for it but to practice and learn, preferably with a knowledgeable helper the first half dozen times at least.

Here's how to do it:

Before you begin, make sure the noseband buckle is open, and also the throatlatch buckle. (It is common in lesson programs for students to slide the bridle off without undoing the noseband buckle. So save yourself some trouble and always check that the noseband is unbuckled before you begin. A fastened noseband will make it even more difficult to the the bit into the horse's mouth.)

Pick up the bridle by the crown piece, making sure you also have hold of the part of the throatlatch (the skinnier strap) that runs beneath it. Keep this in your right hand. Stand close to the horse's head on his left side. Let the reins drop into your left hand and put them up over the horse's head with the bridle facing front, in short, facing the way it will sit on the horse's head. Now transfer the bridle, grasped the same way, into your left hand. Get REALLY REALLY close to the horse's head and reach your right hand under his neck, bringing it up around his face about halfway between his eyes and nose.

Now, transfer the top of the bridle, both straps together, into your right hand. Use your shoulder to keep the horse's head close and in position, and your left hand to gently guide the bit until it is right under and between the horse's lips. DO NOT FORCE THE BIT INTO HIS MOUTH WITH YOUR HAND! Rather, using your left hand as a guide and keeping it far from the teeth, pull the right hand up along the horse's face until you can slip the crownpiece (with throatlatch) over his ears. Push the ears through the crownpiece by pushing or folding them forward, never backward as that is painful to the horse.

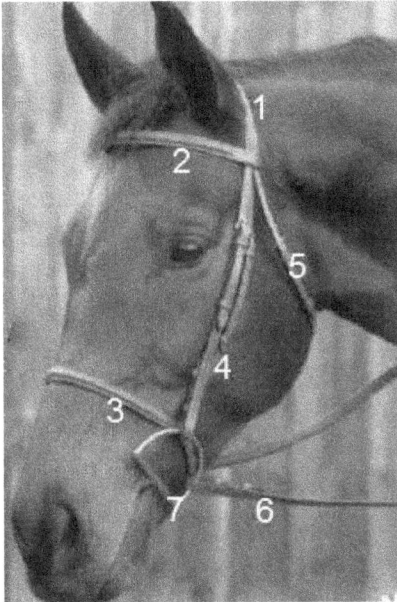

The parts of the bridle:
1. Crownpiece
2. Brow band
3. Noseband
4. Cheek piece
5. Throatlatch
6. Reins
7. Bit, in this case a D-ring snaffle bit

Now, make sure the noseband strap is beneath the cheek pieces on each side of the face and buckle the noseband under the chin. You should make it tight enough that you can get one finger easily between the horse's chin and the noseband.

Next, buckle the throatlatch. It is buckled properly if you can put four fingers laid flat between the lower edge of the curve of his jaw and the throatlatch.

Now, you're ready to lead the horse out to be ridden.

Handling Your Horse

The most basic part of handling your horse is leading him. If you take lessons at a lesson barn or riding academy, they will probably show you how to lead your horse while teaching you to tack up. Some, however, present saddled horses to the students, so the student need only lead the horse to the mounting area by the reins. Leading a horse with a lead rope and halter presents a bit more challenge; there is no bit in the horse's mouth to remind him to behave. The handler must correct any missteps through proper actions alone.

How to lead a horse

Some lesson barns and riding academies leave halters on their horses virtually all the time. In that case, all you will have to do is hook up the lead rope to the loose ring under the horse's chin.

However, if you need to halter the horse first, here's how it's done:

Halters have a buckle at the top holding the crownpiece—the part that goes over the horse's head behind the ears—and many also have a snap on the cheek piece that makes it easier to get the halter on and off than using the buckle. (Not all do, however.) If the halter has a snap, unsnap it. If it doesn't, undo the buckle.

Pick the halter up with your right hand at the crownpiece with the front facing the same direction as the horse's head. How can you tell? Quite frankly, this can be tricky, especially if someone has messed the halter up or flung it around when they took it off. The bottom of the halter will have a noseband that forms a complete circle. In the middle of the bottom of that circle will be another strap that attaches to the strap that goes under the horse's throat and ends up in either the snap end or an end with holes in it to attach the buckle.

Stand next to the horse's head. Transfer the halter to your left hand by the crownpiece, and reach your right hand under the horse's neck. Transfer the crownpiece back to your right hand, position the noseband under the horse's muzzle, and pull up around the lower part of his face. Slide the halter over his ears while bending the ears forward, not back, so that the crownpiece lies behind the ears and temporarily holds the halter in place until you can get the snap or buckle fastened. Step aside and turn slightly to face the horse, keeping the lower part of the cheek piece in your left hand, bringing it up to attach to the upper part of the cheek piece, whether a snap or buckle closure, with your right hand.

If you need to put the horse on crossties, use the rings on the noseband, not the upper ones where the cheek-piece meets the crownpiece. If you are ready to lead the horse, snap the lead rope—a six- or eight-foot nylon, cotton rope or leather 'leash'—to the loose ring under the chin. If you need to tie the horse to a single ring in the wall, use the loose ring and use a quick release knot positioned so that the horse's nose is about two feet from the wall.

Following is a diagram of how a quick-release knot is tied:

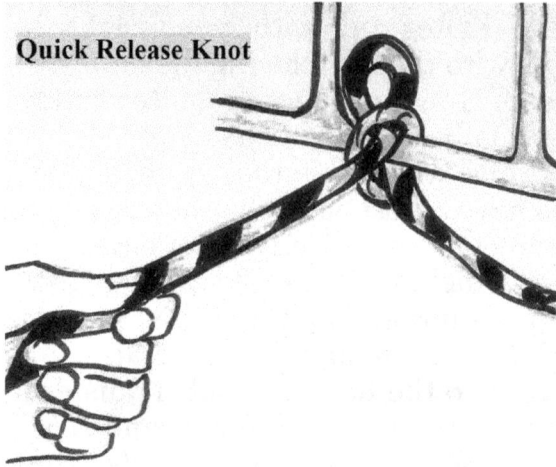
Quick Release Knot

When a horse has been bridled, leave the reins draped over his neck until you are ready to lead him. At that time, stand next to the horse's left shoulder or neck and pass the reins back over his head and grasp both reins together with your right hand about eight inches below his chin around both reins at once. Remain on the horse's left, or near, side.

Take the long, loose end in the left hand about eight inches from the end of the reins, where the buckle is, and grasp both reins. Your right hand may be raised a bit, depending on the height of the horse and your height; your left hand should be comfortably low beside your hips. The reins will pass in front of your body in a bit of a curve.

Warning! Never wind reins or lead ropes around your hands!

That bears repeating:

**Never wind reins or lead ropes around your hands...
Or any other part of your body.**

You must always be able to simply open the palm of your hand and drop the rope or reins when you are leading a horse. If something truly frightens him and he bolts, *just let him go*, and call out "Loose horse!" so that others can step aside and/or close gates and/or help you catch him. Remember, if a horse gets loose, you can always catch him again. *You can't, however, if you have been dragged after him.*

If you're an adult, your one- or two-hundred pounds are no match for his thousand. Even if you think you are a tough guy. A child's 80 pounds? No way.

What if you and your horse are home alone? Still, do not endanger yourself. Let the horse go. If you can yell or phone for help, do so; maybe someone can shut the gate for you if it is open (it shouldn't be), or bring a small bucket of grain to entice an excited horse so he can be caught. If not, enlist help from neighbors and understand that you may just have an afternoon's exercise following your horses over the fields or down the roadways. Remember to bring a halter and lead rope with you, and perhaps a pocketful of grain to entice him.

About the near side and off side:

By now, you've noticed the terms Near and Off. The left side of the horse is the NEAR side; the right side of the horse is the OFF side. All work with horses begins and ends on the NEAR side, including grooming, leading him, mounting and dismounting.

These 'sides' were identified centuries ago, and most horses are trained to know that they are mounted always from the near side. Some trainers also make sure a horse is trained to accept mounting and dismounting from the off side; others don't, and some horses don't like being mounted from the wrong side. You can't tell which ones will tolerate it without being told.

Simply training yourself to always mount from the near side eliminates the problem. When you have your own horse, it will be useful to train him to accept mounting either way.

Why? You may be in a spot in a field when you need to remount and that's the only convenient side to do it from for some reason or another. Or you may sustain an injury from some activity in your life that makes it painful for you to mount from the near side; if you can ride despite the injury, then mounting from the off side would be a convenience.

When you are ready to lead the horse, step forward, and say, "Walk." If the horse does not immediately follow with his head or neck approximately at your shoulder, give one sharp tug on the reins as you say, "Walk."

Do not walk ahead of your horse. Walk at his shoulder, or neck, or head. Then, you can monitor his reactions and attitudes and take corrective or evasive action as needed. If your horse is following you at the end of a led rope, you have little idea what he's thinking about, and even less hope of controlling his gait or his behavior. You are also in danger of being pushed or knocked over if he is frightened before you could either shank him (give a hard, downward tug on the lead to correct him), or get out of the way if a shanking would be insufficient to control him.

Do not turn to look at him. Horses regard this as a confrontational move, and may even back up. (Aggressive horses, which you should not be dealing with right now anyway, may regard this as an invitation to invade your space, or even to charge.) If he is still reluctant, use you right hand to give him a sharp smack on the shoulder, then quickly regain the reins and give a tug and say, "Walk." Any horse you are dealing with at this point should comply. If he doesn't, call your instructor or a more experienced rider for help.

When you arrive at your destination, stop walking, give a small backward tug on the reins with your right hand, and say, "Whoa." It is pronounced without the W or A, as a more drawn out version of Santa Claus's laugh: Hoh.

How to ask a horse to stand for mounting

When you have stopped the horse at your destination, probably the mounting block, you'll need to set him up for mounting.

After he has stopped in the proper place, move around in front of him and gently slip the reins over his head. (If you are short and the horse is tall, take the reins in your hands as if they were a jump rope and swing them up and over the horse's head in a single smooth motion.

Now move back to his near side, and grasp the closest reins in your left hand at the level of the withers. Put your right hand against his shoulder and tell him to "Stand." If he swings his rear end around toward you, step toward his rear and push it away, with a fair amount of pressure, with your right hand, maintaining the reins in your left.

If he swings his rear end away, you'll have to move around in front of the horse to his off side, switching the hold on the reins to your right hand as you go, and pushing with your left hand against his rear end. When you push, target the large, flat area below the point of his hip, which you should be able to determine as a hard bump toward the top of the rear end. There is often a visible shallow hollow at this point. Push there and say, "Move over," firmly.

About the voice and horses: Some horses know actual words. Others respond to your tone and timbre. When talking to horses regarding their work for you, the best voice to use is one in your deeper register (not artificially so, but the voice you would use if someone told you to lower your voice in a social situation), and a medium cadence. In short, give instructions and convey by your matter-of-fact tone that you expect results.

If you are frightened, the horse will hear it and get frightened as well, making everything worse. So, if you're frightened, don't whistle a happy tune, but rather make yourself drop your voice and slow it down, which will calm both you and the horse.

Screaming or raising the register of your voice around horses is a bad idea; they react negatively to any hint of fear or crabbiness in humans.

Do not yell or scream around horses; that upsets them. If you become frightened around horses or on their backs—and that isn't unheard of—remember to bring your voice and everything else down a notch, which will help you and the horse deal with whatever is going on. And most importantly, take a deep breath. Or five.

How to adjust the stirrup length

For a long while, if you are taking lessons, your instructor will adjust your stirrups for you. Your job, then, is to raise your leg and move it forward or backward as your instructor asks so the adjustment can be accomplished; the buckle that regulates the length of the stirrup leathers—which hold the stirrup irons to the saddle—hides up under the skirt, the small saddle flap extending from the seat and over the much longer saddle flap.

There is a method for pre-adjusting stirrups, which, for most people, will put them within a comfortable, effective range, and it can be done before you mount. When the horse is properly standing, loop the reins over your left arm in such a way that you could easily let them slip off quickly if the need arose. Still, it allows you to maintain some control while you make the adjustment.

Pull the irons, which will have been tucked up under the skirt, down to the end of the leather. Fully extend your left arm—even though the reins are looped over it—so that you can touch the stirrup bar with the very tips of your fingers. With your right hand, put the bottom of the stirrup iron flat against your left armpit.

If it reaches exactly, the stirrup leathers are probably a decent, if not perfect, length for you. If it falls short, stopping somewhere along the bottom of your upper arm, then you need to lengthen them until the iron fits into your armpit. If the iron more than reaches, you'll have to shorten the leathers by adjusting at the buckle.

To do this, you will have to pull the top leather down until the buckle is far enough away from the stirrup bar to work with. Then, when you've adjusted up or down as many holes as you estimate you need to reach 'armpit' length, pull on the bottom leather until the buckle is back up under the skirt once more.

Depending on whether you are riding forward seat or balanced seat, two forms of hunt seat, the bottom of the stirrup iron should reach just below, at or above your ankle bone when you are seated in the saddle with your legs relaxed and extending straight down.

If you are riding balanced seat, the irons should hit either below or at your ankle, depending on your comfort. You will ride with them at this length until you begin to jump. Then you will raise them to either mid-ankle or slightly above, depending on your comfort. If you are riding forward seat, the irons will remain at the shorter length—at your ankle bone or a little above, depending on comfort—for riding both on the flat and over fences.

Now you're ready to mount your horse.

Chapter Nine: Mounting

Whether your stirrup leathers have been pre-adjusted or not, before you mount, see that your girth is tight.

If it is tight enough, you will have a hard time getting a couple of fingers under it. If you can easily run your fingers under it, it must be tightened. Run the near side stirrup back up to the bar if you've already lowered it, raise the flap of the saddle, and, keeping the reins looped over your left arm, tighten the girth. Then let the stirrup iron back down.

You can mount from the ground or from a mounting block. You should be able to mount from the ground, eventually, on any size horse no matter what your height is. But to begin, you'll want to put as little stress on yourself and on the horse a possible. So, it is best to make yourself artificially taller by using a mounting block.

A mounting block is simply a two-step, very stable stool that you can buy in any tack shop for under $50. They are usually heavy duty– plastic, and they come in a variety of colors. They have wide bases so they won't sink into the sand of an arena—which is why an ordinary household step stool will not do.

If you do not have a mounting block or cannot get one, you can use any other solid, stationary object the horse doesn't mind. Often, people find an old tree stump, either still *in situ* or sawed down and acquired for the purpose, and use that. This is a very unthreatening sort of mounting block for the horse. Horses are used to trees and have no problem standing next to something that looks natural to them.

Sometimes, people use a picnic table, or a set of stairs that is beside the arena, perhaps leading to a judges' stand. Some barns build mounting blocks that are permanently attached to a wall or are very large, immovable and permanent fixtures of the property.

In any case, once you have the horse so that its saddle is parallel to the mounting block with the horse about a foot from it, you are ready to ascend the mounting block and mount the horse.

How to mount

First, go around to the off side of the horse, and be sure the stirrup iron is pulled down. Keep a hand on the reins as you go. Then come back around to the near side, and climb the steps of the mounting block.

With your stomach facing the saddle, grasp the reins so that there is an almost straight line from the horse's mouth to your hand when you also grab a hank of mane in that same hand right in front of the withers. There will be a loop of rein left over. Just let it hang down.

Grasp the cantle with your right hand while still holding the reins.

Put your left foot into the stirrup iron at your foot's widest point, in other words, the ball of your foot.

Count to three, bounce on your right foot with a little give in your knee. On three, bounce off your right foot, straighten your left knee until you have the clearance to swing your right leg over the horse's back between the saddle and his tail (this area is called his croup) without dragging your foot across his skin.

Twist your hips as you go so that when your right leg is at the other side of the horse, you will be facing front.

Then, bending your left knee, gently lower yourself into the deepest part of the saddle.

When you are there, breathe deeply, and find the other stirrup iron with your right toe. You may have to glance down to do it the first dozen times or so, but try it without glancing, as long as you are not poking the horse's side too much.

About grabbing mane: Most beginners think they will hurt the horse if they take a handful of mane and tug on it. It won't hurt him. And the hair doesn't come out that way, either.

It does come out if you take just a couple of hairs at a time, though. But like human hair, which supports circus performers on flying trapezes, horse manes are built to take it. Indeed, they are there for your support when you begin jumping. In some ways, they take the place of the western saddle horn for helping with balance. In fact, they are better than a saddle horn, because mane won't poke you in the stomach if you inadvertently fall forward. And the mane is always there to use, even when you're riding bareback.

If you are mounting from the ground, the procedure is exactly the same, except that you will need more bounce and more muscle to get yourself up...and you've got to be very, very sure the girth is tight enough because it will be taking all your weight; the mounting block mitigates this somewhat.

Some trainers insist on always using mounting blocks; others won't let anyone ride unless they mount from the ground.

Here's the rationale for each belief.

Not using mounting blocks: These instructors do not want the student to be unable to mount without one. But there are times—for instance, with a very short rider and a very tall horse—that even the various tricks of the trade will not work. One of those tricks is to let the stirrup leather on the near side down a good way until the rider can reach it with the left foot. Sometimes, that is so far—depending on the disparity in rider and horse sizes—that the rider almost has to climb hand over hand to mount. That is ridiculous, except under necessity such as having to remount for one reason or another out in the field, and cruel to the horse. Remember, when you mount, you are thrusting your entire weight up onto the horse's spine, and you're doing it by pulling quite hard against his spine and all the muscles running under the girth. The more easily you can accomplish mounting, the better for both of you in the long run.

Always use a mounting block, if one is available: These instructors are protecting their school horses' spines, a very excellent idea. Still, students must know how to accomplish mounting under extreme circumstances, so, occasionally, mounting should be practiced without a mounting block.

Informed opinion: Some instructors insist on not ever using a mounting block; others insist on always using it. For the benefit of the horse, always use a mounting block. But for your own versatility, occasionally mount from the ground just so you know that you can in a pinch.

Getting a leg up

Every rider should know how to get and how to give a leg up. It is a useful tactic for times when you must mount without a block but do have another rider around who is not riding and could help. And sometimes, it would take too long to find a mounting block, for example, when a show is moving faster than expected and you are suddenly the next horse and rider called to the arena. If your instructor or another student can give you a leg up right at the gate, you will avoid being late and annoying the judge and spectators.

To get a leg up, stand facing the horse, with your hands placed as for mounting from a block. Get very close to your horse, even brushing the saddle with the front of your shirt or jacket. Bend your left leg at the knee and stick it out behind you. The person giving the leg up will grasp it to thrust you up. You must keep your leg very stiff and strong from hip joint to knee joint.

On a count of three (preferably yours or yours and your helper's together), you will bounce off your right leg as when using a block and spring into the air as your helper lifts your weight by firmly grasping and pushing up using the lower half of your bent leg to do so. As you do when mounting from a block, you will twist in the air so you can sit facing front after your leg clears the horse's croup.

Since you do not have one foot in a stirrup to soften your landing on the horse's back, do that as much as you can by using your hands on the pommel and cantle as much as possible to soften your descent onto the horse's back.

How to give a leg up

The person giving the leg up has got the harder job, and should take care to lift with the thighs rather than the back. If someone is too heavy for you to lift, especially if that person is too weak to offer much 'bounce', politely decline. Suggest a stump or picnic table to use as a makeshift mounting block if no mounting block is available, and offer to hold the horse while the rider mounts.

But if you are ready, willing and able to give a leg up, here's how it's done:

When the rider is in position, stand next to his or her left leg, facing the horse's rear end. Reach down and grip the lower part of her leg at the calf and just above the ankle with both hands, letting one hand come around from the rear of the leg, the other from the front. Crouch slightly so that you can use your thigh muscles to accomplish the lift. On a mutual count of three, with hands firmly grasping the rider's leg as explained, rise up, taking the rider's leg with you. You do not have to turn;

the rider will do that and, as she or he twists, you will realize it is time to let go of the leg.

Getting and giving a leg up are both fairly difficult tasks, in fact. It demands of the rider's and helper's attention, fellow feeling, strength, athleticism and ability to sense when enough is enough in terms of muscle. However, it is a useful skill to have around horses, for both rider and helpers, and worth learning. Be warned; you may both look a bit like fools the first few times, and the rider may literally be scrambling onto the horse's back if either misjudges distance and muscle required and so on. So make sure your early practice is with 'bombproof' school horses. Those unflappable guys let us practice these things without getting upset and nervous. If you stay relaxed about it, it won't be a bad learning curve at all.

How to place the feet in the stirrups

If you have properly placed your foot in the left stirrup to mount and is hasn't moved, it will be in the right place, pretty much, once you're on. The stirrup leather, which had been lying flat against the horse's side, will now be twisted so that its front edge is pointing away from the horse's side as the leather runs down your leg. When you pick up the other iron, feel around for it with your toe, and then pick it up by turning your foot pigeon-toed toward the horse's side. When the iron has slid under your foot, the leather should also be properly placed, with the front edge of it now pointing away from that side of the horse's body as the leather runs down your leg.

Rest your feet in the irons so that a spot just behind your big toe touches the upright portion of the iron and the ball of your foot rests on the stirrup itself. Now relax your ankle joint, and then, keeping the iron under the ball of your foot, push your heels toward the ground, as if you were walking on your heels. Rest your calves against the side of the horse firmly. Don't squeeze, but maintain firm control.

How to sit in the saddle

Scoot your seat forward so the pommel bumps your pelvis. Incline the top of your hips just slightly in front of the vertical (creating a very slight lordosis in your back, about half of what you see in ballet dancers), and square your shoulders, keeping your chest open wide. Shrug up and drop your shoulder blades behind you; now your arms will hang at your sides in the proper position to begin holding the reins.

Warning! You will have to perform the upper body maneuvers again, probably, once you've picked up your reins.

How to hold the reins

Contrary to popular belief, the reins are not used to hold you on the horse. Your seat, legs and balance do that. Reins are used to direct the horse's movement (in concert with your legs and seat) and to slow or stop the horse (also in concert with legs and seat.)

The way they are held allows good sensory input into your hands so you can feel what the horse is doing, a skill that is developed over time. The way they are held also keeps them from being pulled out of your hands if the horse makes a big head movement, such as a sneeze, for instance.

But what happens then? You might ask: If I don't let go of the reins and he puts his head down in a big sneeze, won't he pull me over his head? He could, except that you have elbows. So when a horse makes a big head movement, keep the grasp on the reins, and allow your elbows to open and straighten out your arms to accommodate the movement. If that's not enough, let your torso go forward slightly, as well. But don't let go of those reins!

If you do, you will have nothing with which to stop the horse if he decides to walk away.

To hold the reins properly, stick out your hand as if you were going to do the chug-chug motion playing choo-choo train. Slap your hand down flat over the rein as it lies on the horse's neck. Now curl all four fingers around the rein and grasp it and lift it up so you can finish getting the reins. At this point, the rein will be coming from the bit, through your fist from the bottom, and out the top between your index finger and thumb. Let the rein lie over the first segment of your index finger, and mash it down with your thumb. Don't do it with your thumb straight but rather hump the thumb up so you can hold it with the soft, fleshy part of your thumb. (And besides, that will prevent breaking a nail if your hand contacts the horse's neck!) A good test to see if your thumbs are placed correctly is this: you should be able to see the ridge where your thumb bends, but not the fingernail.

Almost finished. Now just sneak your pinky finger out from around the rein, and tuck it in below the rein. Why? Because when you get to an upper level and are riding more demanding horses, you may need double reins. In that case, the second rein takes that spot under your pinky before going up through your closed hand with the other rein.

About reins: The regular rein is a snaffle rein, or just 'the reins' in a single-rein bridle. In a double-rein bridle, the regular rein or snaffle rein goes where it goes now. The second rein, or curb rein, is the one that goes beneath your pinky. Often, it is a slightly different width than the snaffle rein to make it easier to know which rein is where without looking.

Informed opinion: There are two schools of thought about double reins. Some instructors prefer the curb rein to replace the snaffle rein, with the snaffle carried under the pinky. However, this causes the reins to cross each other on their way from the bit to the rider's hand, meaning the horse no longer feels a straight pull on his mouth. In addition, because the ring finger is used to exerting all the pressure, it is likely that a rider will use the curb rein too often and too hard in this arrangement.

Now you'll have to adjust the length of the reins. Ideally, there should be a straight line from the horse's mouth along the reins and your lower arm to your elbow. When you begin, this should be a gentle straight line, without making harsh contact with the mouth. When you first pick up the reins, they will probably be too long, though. To adjust them, move your hands next to each other and use the thumb of one hand to pull the rein up through the fist of the other hand, releasing your finger and thumb pressure on that rein just enough to accomplish that. Then fix the opposite rein.

If you need to lengthen the reins, simply release a little pressure and move your hand along the leather until it is closer to the buckle, which will be in the middle of the reins.

Extra rein should loop down the off side of the horse's neck, out of your way.

About your wrists: Wrists should always be held straight so that you can always see the knuckle of your thumbs. They should not be bent to the inside or the outside and should never be cocked upward or downward. Think of holding a pistol on a shooting range, and you'll have a picture of the approximate way your wrists should be...always.

How to dismount

There are two ways to dismount. One is more elegant; the other is, in my opinion, safer.

The more elegant way is the step-off dismount.

The safer way is the vault-off dismount.

You may wish to know both. Vaulting off is preferable with a horse that tends to bolt or is a bit excitable. Stepping off is fine for all other horses (although ANY HORSE may do ANY THING at ANY TIME without warning, simply because it is a horse). And a step-off is useful to know in the event that you develop a physical problem that makes vaulting hard on you.

When you ride a horse, balance comes not from freezing your legs to the saddle, but from learning to float with the movement of the horse as you ride. Each step is a dance, the rider's dance as well as the dance of the horse.
—Chogyam Trungpa Rinpoche, Tibetan meditation master (1939–1987)

Practice mounting and dismounting several times before you actually begin to ride the horse at a walk.

Vault-off dismount

When the horse is standing still, gather both reins in your left hand and also grab a hank of mane. Slip both feet out of the stirrup irons. Lean forward over the horse's neck. Supporting your weight on your left hand and stomach/chest, swing your right leg up and over the horse's croup. As it clears, swing your torso around so that your face is looking over the off side of the horse. Simultaneously grasp the cantle with your right hand. As your weight shifts to the near side of the horse, slide gently down the saddle, helping yourself with both hands, until your feet touch the ground. Or, if you are more energetic, give a small push with your hands and spring slightly away from the horse, landing on your feet. Remember to absorb the shock of landing on slightly bended knees.

Step-off dismount

When the horse is standing still, gather both reins in your left hand and also grab a hank of mane. Take only your right foot out of the stirrup iron. Grasp both reins in your left hand. Straighten your left leg until you are almost standing in the iron; at the same time, swing your right leg over the croup. As it comes across, as soon as you can, grasp the cantle with your right hand, continuing to use the mane for support with your left hand, which retains the reins. Now lean your weight onto the saddle using your upper thighs against the saddle for support. Supporting yourself with your thighs and both hands, slip the left foot out of the stirrup iron and slowly lower your weight to the ground, using the hands on the saddle and counterbalancing with your weight pressing against the horse's side as you descend.

Confession: I was taught to vault off, so early and so often that, to this day, I cannot bring myself to step off. While I believe that vaulting off is safer at all times, stepping off is a useful skill for any rider, and should be both taught and practiced in safe conditions.

Chapter Ten: Walk and Halt

Getting on the horse doesn't mean you've gotten anywhere. Some horses are so lazy they'd stand there all day unless asked to do otherwise. Others, of course, are raring to go...but you wouldn't be on one of those for your beginning rides, anyway.

Clearly, the next order of business is to get the horse to move. And no, you don't say, "Yo, dude, move it." In fact, with horses—except if they are being unruly—you always ask rather than tell. When handling horses, tact is very important. Despite the cowboy movies you've seen, horses respond much better to being asked things in a calm, expectant manner rather than an aggressive, bullying one. Good thing, too. You couldn't outbully or outmuscle a horse if you tried. So be grateful that they respond best to what I like to call it the velvet fist in the iron glove.

This is not a brainteaser. It is just a way to think about horses. They are huge beasts so you must be firm and more forceful with them than you would be with the family cat. At the same time, they have been called (and I believe they are) very spiritual beings, so at the core of your attitude toward them must be kindness and love. Combine those two things—a firm demeanor arising out of unconditional love and tactful treatment—and 99.99 percent of your dealings with horses are likely to be positive ones.

About communicating with your horse: Whenever you want a horse to do something, you first ask, then insist, and then demand.

Confirm your own position first

Before you ask a horse to walk, check your own position, as described in Chapter Nine: Mounting.

First, check your stirrup length. With legs out of stirrups and hanging relaxed down horse's side, see that the bottom of the stirrup iron is at your anklebone or just below or just above it, depending on comfort. (The preference is just above the ankle for forward seat, just below for balanced seat.)

Now pick up your irons; that is, *without looking*, find them with your feet and slide your feet into them.

Take inventory of your position, beginning at the bottom. See that:

•The balls of your feet are in the stirrup irons, heels pointing down as far as possible without causing yourself pain or beginning a stretch you cannot sustain for half an hour to an hour.

•Your stirrup leathers are solid against your legs with the front edge pointing away from the horse as the leather travels down your leg.

•Your calf muscle is solid against horse's side.

•Your knees are bent and pointing forward and laying flat against the saddle.

•You are sitting forward in the saddle so that your pelvis touches the pommel.

•The tops of your hips are pointing slightly forward to create a slight lordosis, very slight, in concert with squared shoulders.

Action steps

When your basic position is good, shrug upward and let your shoulders drop down behind to open your chest. Let your arms hang from your shoulders in a relaxed manner, elbows slightly in front of your torso and bent to create a straight line from your elbow, along your forearm, through your straight wrist and down the reins to the horse's mouth.

See that your chin is level and your gaze is in the direction you want to go. But don't stare. Begin to learn the concept that Sally Swift calls 'soft eyes' in her book, *Centered Riding*. You will look where you want to go, but you will train yourself to be calmly aware of what is in your peripheral vision area at the same time.

Make sure your hip joints are loose, and ready to move in concert with the movement of the saddle when the horse steps off. The first time you ride, you will be surprised at how much movement is happening under you. In fact, because of that—and before you begin to practice the walk—you need to learn to halt.

But first, you have to learn to stop him. If that seems like putting the first things last, it would be, except that, on horseback, you can't read the instructions and if you're alone, you can't ask anyone, either. So, a little practice in halting should precede a little practice in going forward.

How to halt a horse

Fortunately, halting a horse is easy—as easy as anything is with horses.

To halt, sit deep in the saddle, stop the motion of your hips, press both calves into his sides a little, and squeeze back on the reins. Add a 'whoa' if you need it.

To practice, just go through the motions on your recently mounted horse. Because he is already at 'halt,' he might take a step or two backwards. Good; you'll know you're on the right track. Just release your reins and relax your hips and legs until he stops going backward.

Here's how to apply a halt once you are going forward:

Make the decision to halt, and decide where. As you approach that spot, stiffen your lower back slightly so your hips stop following the horse. Your horse will feel the resistance and slow down. Now pull back on the reins toward your hips and absolutely no higher than your waist. If you find you cannot get any 'tug' without raising your hands higher or pulling them behind yourself or leaning back, your reins are way too long. Shorten them and try again.

Warning! Pulling upward on the reins can be very dangerous. The bit will hurt the roof of the horse's mouth and, to avoid the pain, he may do the only thing that makes sense to him: In short, he may rear. While bucking is disconcerting and may cause a fall of the rider, a rear is dangerous. A horse has a hard time balancing on only his hind legs and can fall over backwards on top of the rider.

Experienced riders who feel the start of a rear for any reason (untrained horse, scary situation, rider error) will fling their weight forward, shove their hands and reins forward, and kick the horse hard to bring his front feet back into contact with the ground. Beginners have neither the feel nor the tools for that. So the obvious solution is not to even entertain the possibility. In other words, while you're on a horse's back, NEVER raise your hands higher than your waist.

School horses, generally speaking, will not rear. For one thing, they have been chosen because they do not exhibit this vice,♥ at least at reputable establishments. And often, they are quite old and would have a hard time getting their front feet more than a few inches off the ground, especially with weight on their backs. But still, a horse is a horse, and all horses can do what horses can do if driven beyond their training to their natural state. Fear and pain can do that. So inflict as little pain as possible. Always. But especially when you are a beginner.

♥ A vice, in equine parlance, is not drinking, smoking or gambling. It is doing something, usually habitually that can hurt rider or horse or both. Rearing, if a horse does it more than once in its life with a rider board, is clearly a vice. Cribbing, that is, chewing on stall boards, is also a vice. Cribbing costs money by damaging stalls; however, many cribbers also lose weight and condition, preferring cribbing to eating properly. Some believe that, in fact, horses crib to hyperventilate and produce a 'high' of sorts, much as smoking marijuana does for humans.

124

A better halt

While halting a horse is simple, a good halt is harder to accomplish than a good transition to the walk because you must engage everything you do at the walk, but add resistance.

A beginner's biggest mistake is usually in failing to use leg pressure to accomplish a halt. Since you use leg pressure to go forward, it seems wrong to use it to stop, even though it isn't.

Here's how it works: Taking your legs off the horse's side makes the horse think you're abandoning him. Your legs not only convey what you want the horse to do; they give him a significant source of mental support as well as physical encouragement. Some horses halted without 'leg' will fall apart, literally swing their hind ends around. It's not dangerous, but it is uncomfortable and doesn't look very nice, either. And it risks injury to the horse; the horse has abandoned being athletic, and he still does have a hundred extra pounds or more on his back to balance. He needs to keep his muscles engaged even when halting and standing.

How to ask a horse to walk

It's simple to ask a horse to walk: It's difficult to do it right. Beginning riders often fear to use too much force, so they don't use enough. There's no way around that; each rider has to find the level of 'ask' that works, and often must discover it again with each horse. However, the process itself requires very few steps. Here it is:

Look in the direction you'd like to go.

Release your hands forward slightly.

Press against the horse's sides equally with calf muscles of both legs. (If he's really lazy, also say "Walk," or cluck. A cluck is NOT the kissing sound western riders use to encourage a horse onward, but rather a cluck like a chicken makes.)

Guess what? The first time you do this—and maybe the 50th time—your horse probably will not go. He's not stupid. He knows you're a beginner and he'll avoid working as long as you let him.

So...start again. Press harder with the calf muscles and do all the rest.

He still won't go.

By this time, you're tempted to flap the reins at him, another thing you might have seen in western movies. Don't do it. Don't ever do it. First of all, it doesn't work. In fact, it has the opposite effect because, to a horse, pulling on the reins mean slow down or stop. And you could easily hurt his mouth by jerking the bit around. And then he might get really silly, and try to run away from you (except you're going to be running with him unless you fall off...but horses aren't smart enough to know that.)

You might be tempted to get active with your body and bounce around in the seat, but that might hurt the horse's back. If he does move forward, it would be only to avoid pain. And, as above, he might decide to run away from you.

Eeek! Now what?

Kick.

Don't kick like you're looking for a field goal. But use both feet and tap both the horse's sides at the same time. More than 99 times out of a hundred, he will walk. In fact, since he has been stuck in one place and so have you, he might lurch you around a little as he moves suddenly into a walk. Don't worry about it. Breathe, and adjust your kick next time. Use it earlier—after no more than two ineffective presses—and adjust its severity.

When a horse walks, he uses his head and neck and he will pull the reins through your hands unless you keep your fingers tightly closed. But compensate by allowing your elbows to close and open in concert with the motion of his head.

Here's a way to think about it: You get to keep your fingers the way you want them, tightly closed on the reins for safety and control, and the horse gets to have your elbows the way he wants them, loose and following his mouth.

It's a simple equation:

Fingers=yours. Elbows=the horse's.

Getting used to this concept and the motion now will help you out later on, when you begin to canter.

How to steer

There are three main aids for steering: legs, hands and eyes. When you get more advanced, your seat and hips will also be useful. But for now, these three are enough to learn.

There is, however, one other crucial element to steering; decision. Decide where you want the horse to go, and half the battle is won.

Once you've decided, use your eyes to look in the direction you want to travel. If you want to go to the right, move your right hand away from the horse's neck, level with its proper position just at or slightly in front of the withers. (This is called a leading rein, not surprisingly. Later, you will learn an indirect rein technique. But to start, keep it simple and effective.)

At the same time, push against the horse's side with your left leg. You pull him in the direction you want to travel, and push him at the same time. Keep your eyes on the place you'd like to end up. Your eyes will also move your head, and horses can feel quite well the movement of a human's head, and will respond by wondering why the human is looking that way, and will also look that way, making it easier to get him to go that way.

Obviously, if you wanted the horse to move toward the left, you would look to the left, move your left hand away from the neck keeping your hand at a consistent level (this is called a leading or opening rein) and push against him with your right leg.

Do not ask for any of these directional movements until the horse begins to walk; if you do, you might compare it to turning a parked car, and you'll get about the same results. That is, lots of work for virtually no reward.

So start the walk first, then, a few steps out, begin moving the horse right or left, as needed, to get where you want to go.

If you are riding in an arena, eventually, you'll come to a corner.

How to ride a corner

On the straight side, be sure your horse is moving forward. Tap him or press him with your legs until you get a walk that is forward enough so that your relaxed hips swing in the saddle with the movement.

As you approach the corner, gaze into the corner. About twenty feet from the place where the lines of fence meet, begin putting a little more pressure against the horse's side with the leg toward the open space of the arena, the inside leg. Allow your outside hip to go forward slightly, keeping your leg position. Allow your inside shoulder to come back slightly as you press in with your inside leg.

As you continue to approach the corner, without twisting your head (which should still be looking ahead between the horse's ears), glance through the corner and out the other side. You will make your body and your horse's body follow your eyes out of the corner.

It will take a bit of practice to make all these things work together every time. It will take lots of riding to make them second nature, but that's the intent and it's never too soon to begin.

A refinement to this is moving your outside lower leg back just an inch or so, still keeping its downward position, to help the horse use his hind legs in the corners, too. But don't add this until you've got the basics down. Here's a corner-riding checklist:

- Prepare with your eyes 20 feet or so from the corner.
- Begin to press the horse's side with your inside leg, and increase pressure in the corner.
- Allow your outside hip to turn slightly so that it is in front of your inside hip just a little, mimicking the bend in the horse's body.
- Allow your inside shoulder to drift back.

Practice the corners in both directions equally, for your muscular development and that of the horse. This helps keep your reins even outside and inside. The horse's body gets 'shorter' on the inside and 'longer' on the outside. When your outside hip goes forward, it takes your torso and arm along with it, following the greater outside arc. When your inside shoulder comes back, it takes your arm with it so that you won't end up with a loopy rein on the 'shorter' inside arc. This also helps the horse know where he is to put his body without kicking, pulling and tugging.

Think of all this like a long balloon. As you twist the balloon into a C shape, the outside of the C stretches or expands, while the inside is compressed.

As you ride out of the corner, square your shoulders again, use equal leg pressure on each side of the horse, and ride down the long side, sending your eyes ahead of you toward the next corner.

About eyes: Using your eyes for riding requires seeing the surrounding panorama, but also the point you wish to reach. Avoid over-focusing your eyes on a single point, but rather, mentally 'mark' it within your entire field of vision.

This is simple, but it isn't easy. You are learning a whole new 'body language,' and with it, you are also trying to control a horse that has its own mind and body language. It may take you 50 corners to really feel comfortable about what you're doing, and to relax enough for the horse to relax, too.

Don't be surprised if there is a lack of impulsion—that is, your horse slows down—as you begin to practice this technique. You are experimenting and unsure, and he feels that.

Once you've got the technique down, then work at keeping the same pace into, through and out of the corner.

School horses are chosen for their ability to tolerate your learning curve. If you've bought a horse, you should have bought a similar type. And, working on your own, remember that you may be wildly enthused about continuing the exercise until you get it exactly right. But in horsemen's terms, you don't want to fry your horse's brain about it. What's interesting to you gets boring for him. When you suspect this is the case—or after about 20 minutes at any one thing, tops—do something else, or call it a day, give him a carrot and let him go back to being a horse; groom him and turn him out to play.

Warning! School horses, because they do the same things over and over, do get bored. And having slightly simple brains, they assume they will get done faster if they literally cut corners. So it may be extra hard, with an experienced school horse, to get him into those corners. Until he knows you mean business about it, you may have to use an opening rein—moving your outside hand a good distance away from his neck while pressing extra hard with your inside leg. And he still may avoid it, until you get some more experience at it. The horse is not being bad; he's just being a school horse who thinks he knows more than you do, and he does, at least about the little 'school horse' tricks he has gotten by with in the past.

During all of this, and the next exercises, remember to:

BREATHE...BREATHE...BREATHE

About corners: When you ride in an arena, you would think a horse would just naturally turn corners, rather than bump into the fence. And to a point, that's true. But there are good corners and bad corners; there are corners the way you want to ride them, and the way your horse wants to go. Since you are the 'brains of the outfit,' the choice should be yours.

Here is what makes a good corner, and why:

One: A good corner is ridden at exactly the same pace into, through and out of it.

Two: It hugs the fence line, making a deep arc to actually get through the corner.

Three: The horse's body bends through the corner.

Four: The rider's body also changes position through the corner, with hips, hands and shoulders following the horse's curve through the corner.

All this is necessary for the physical well being of the horse (the more he uses himself athletically, the better developed his muscles will be, and the longer useful, happy lifespan he is likely to have, all other things being equal.) It is also necessary for the rider in order to set herself up for the next maneuver, if that eventually involves things like coming out of the corner to jump a fence, and just to set up a nice, straight walk down the other side of the arena...to the next corner.

And it is necessary in a show. If two riders/horses are equally attractive to the judge in what they do and what they are, riding good corners can be one of the tiebreakers. So you might as well start now to get those little details working in your favor just in case you decide to show, or just to become an accomplished rider, no matter what your riding goals and choices are.

How to reverse direction

There are a number of acceptable ways to change direction. Here, we will learn only the most basic, a simple change of direction on the rail, called a reverse.

Simple change of direction

To accomplish this, you will need the same skills you worked on for cornering. The aim is to turn the horse in the other direction in the same gait at the same speed he is using now, in this case, a good, forward walk.

Here's how: Proceed up the long side of the arena. When you are more than halfway down the fence line, and your see quite a lot of open space without jumps, begin your turn. If you are traveling to the left, which means your left hand is toward the open space to the inside of the arena, glance back over your left shoulder, letting your left hand move back toward your hip. Let your hip turn slightly also. Push against your horse with the inside leg, in this case, the left leg. Let the outside leg drift forward to help his front end around the turn. Because that's all you're doing; you're 'cornering' without a corner. It is almost a full circle you'll make, though, to get back to the rail in the other direction, so all the movements you practiced in cornering are increased in size and pressure at this point.

The horse should now be beginning to move in an arc away from the rail. If you don't want him to go straight across the arena, you'll need to look hard at a spot on the rail about 30 feet from where you are now. Using your inside hand by pulling it back toward your hips more, and your outside leg to push a little toward the front of the saddle, work the horse around the arc, and then straighten out gradually so that he walks a diagonal path back to the fence, where you will once again get everything square and walk on.

In brief:

Choose an open space about 2/3 of the way along the long side of the arena.

Glance over your inside shoulder (left shoulder if you are walking left and want to change to right, and vice versa)

Let your inside arm come back with your shoulder, keeping your hands closed on the reins so the horse will feel the direction you want him to go

Press into the horse with your inside leg.

Move your outside hip and leg forward slightly to help the horse bring his front end around.

Walk him forward at an angle toward the fence at the end of the shallow half-circle you have created, adjusting with both legs and hands to keep him straight.

Square everything up again (shoulders, hips, legs, hands) when you are at the track you've been using along the fence.

Below is a diagram of a reverse:

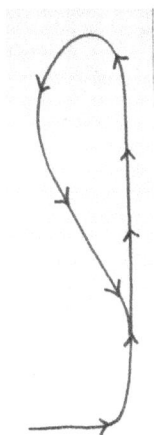

Again, practice in both directions. But don't bore your horse just because you're seeking perfection in a single session; it may take several to master the change of direction. But as always, relax and **BREATHE**.

As physically, mentally and emotionally demanding as learning to ride is—albeit fun!—it 'ain't brain surgery.'

Exercises at walk and halt

Now you know how to ask a horse to walk and get a result, and how to ask him to halt and get a result. You can change directions and practice in both directions. Here is an exercise you can do to strengthen your use of the aids and make the transition to walk or halt smoother.

Ask the horse to walk forward by using a mild kick. Allow him to walk about halfway down the side of the arena. Then ask for a halt. Try to use more seat and less hand. So, before you want the halt, sit 'heavy' on your horse, then close the leg and pull back.

When he has stood still for three seconds or so, ask for the walk again, but ask using slightly less pressure or kick than before. If he doesn't respond, go back to the amount of strength you used when you did get the desired result. Then bring him back to a halt using more seat and less hand than you did the time before.

Repeat this walk to halt to walk exercise, increasing your use of subtle aids (pressing rather than kicking to start the walk, sitting rather than pulling back hard to get the halt) each time. This is a progression from harsher, more obvious technique to kinder, more elegant technique. Increasing kindness—tact—and elegance is how you become both a more effective rider and a more attractive rider to watch, as well as a more welcome rider to your horses.

Do not stop and start at the same place in the arena each time; horses learn by repetition and the horse will begin to make the transitions automatically if he does it more than once or twice at exactly the same spot. And that won't teach you anything about the amount of pressure to use and so on. Quit the exercise before either of you gets bored, but do try to accomplish a net improvement in your technique, no matter how small.

And remember the carrot for the horse after you work him.

About treats: Some barns prohibit giving their horses treats. Some barns require that you put bits of carrot or apple in the horse's feed bucket, and old horsemen will tell you to do this because, they say, hand-feeding makes horses 'mouthy,' that is, prone to bite.

I agree only partially. I have hand-fed all my horses and never had one get 'mouthy' on me. On the other hand, I've seen horses that were just plain 'mouthy' from the start, and continued to be even after all treats were delivered in the feed bucket. So I would say use common sense: Ask the barn or owner about each horse or their general rules, and follow their rules and advice.

If you are allowed to feed treats after a ride, do so right after you remove the bit and put the halter on. The closer to the lesson, the more the horse is likely to associate the treat with a job well done.

When feeding carrots, either get baby carrots, or break big carrots into four or five pieces. Put each piece on the flat palm of your hand and offer it up to the horse to snuffle with his big, soft lips. Reach up far enough that he doesn't have to stretch down or tug against the crossties.

If you feed apples, NEVER give a horse a whole, or even half, apple. It can get lodged in their throat and suffocate them. Cut the apple into quarters and feed the same way as carrot pieces. (If you forget to do this before you go to the barn, you can use the point of a hoof pick to split and re-split the apple into feeding bites.) Never give a horse more than two small or one large apple at a time. Apples can cause gastric difficulties if the horse eats too many at once. On the other hand, carrots are related to asafetida, a plant used to calm stomach upset, so horses can have lots of carrots. In some barns, they may get six or seven in a day from various riders and it doesn't hurt them.

Another treat you can give is a sugar cube. The advantage is that you can keep a box of them in the car or your grooming box so you will always have a treat on hand without remembering to pack the carrots. Horses do like them, but carrots are better for them, of course.

Some horses also like red and white or green and white round hard peppermints. Some don't. Try it, though, if the barn permits. And those, too, are easy to keep a supply of without refrigeration in case you have no carrots or apples on hand.

My horse loves caramel corn and oats and honey granola bars.

Don't give a horse chocolate. Chocolate is toxic to horses, although feeding a horse a candy bar is not likely to affect him much. After all, he weighs 1,000 pounds. But because horses can't metabolize it very well, the caffeine and theobromine in chocolate will show up in blood tests as much as a day later. Since caffeine and theobromine are classified as performance enhancers, illegal in racing but also in horse showing, a horse that had eaten chocolate could be disqualified from a win in a show; it has happened more than once.

New Age Thought for Old World Skills

In the old days, people rode because it was a much better, faster way to get somewhere than walking. These days, we ride because we love the animals, the exercise, the sport, the competition, or the chance to get out into nature on a natural conveyance. We ride, too, for the human companionship and camaraderie among riders. But it is the companionship with the horse itself that becomes most meaningful to most riders, even if it doesn't start out that way. (Some are drawn by the thrill of jumping, or the need to compete in an unusual sport.)

It is never too soon to begin making yourself into the classical image, a horse-person; the ability to become as much one with the horse as it is possible to be while you have your human body to house your spirit and the horse has his equine one.

You can begin to make this connection at the walk by using mindfulness techniques, once you are comfortable enough with physical techniques to take your mind and spirit elsewhere.

The first mindfulness technique you might try is this: At the walk, soften your eyes—that is, allow them to unfocus slightly and take in more of what is beside, below and above you. When you do this, you will be experiencing something more akin to the way horses observe their world than the way humans with our tight focus generally do.

> **The horse will leap over trenches, will jump out of them will do anything else, provided one grants him praise and respite from his accomplishments.**
>
> —Xenophon, ancient Greek soldier, horseman and writer (circa 4th century B.C.)

A second one is to listen to the horse's breathing as he walks and try to relax your own physical rhythms to that cadence.

If you do these two things, you will begin to realize that you are being permitted to ride atop a powerful natural beast that seems actually to be fairly happy in his work.

Would you be as happy with weight on your back directing your movement? Probably not. Naturally, you have a much larger brain, but let's face it, the horse has a much larger body and you couldn't really force him to do this unless he wanted to at some level. The horse is doing this for you. That makes him your best friend, at least at the moment.

Now, connect with the horse physically as closely as you do with your family dog. Bend forward at the waist or hips, and lie right down on the horse's mane. If you are feeling brave, lay the reins on his neck and, for a moment, reach down and hug him around his neck as you walk.

Sit back up and let the reins slip through your hand to the buckle. Lean back as far as you dare, sliding one hand along his back across the croup and as close to the dock, the place where his tail hangs, as you can.

Doing these exercises will supple you for riding, and they will also begin to banish any distrust you might have for horses.

All this is not to say that horses cannot and will not do things that, to us, are stupid or dangerous. But it will help you to understand that the horse is a sovereign beast that cooperates with us in extraordinary ways and can give us extraordinary experiences. The fact that we must take care around them is mainly due to their great size and speed, and not to any animosity they bear us. With very, very few exceptions, horses do not want to hurt humans. If they do, it is generally because they are acting instinctively out of fear, in short, doing just what we do when we are afraid. The difference is that they are a different species and so we don't fully understand that and certainly, we cannot do what they do. (Many of us would love to be able to take off on our own feet at 23 miles per hour if something truly scared us!)

And that brings us to the next, and very important, bit of information ...

When in doubt

Halt. Just halt. If you are afraid because of something the horse is doing or because you are doing something you think might be wrong, or if something in the environment is frightening you, halt. It is always a proper response in order to assess a situation, or to ask for help or even dismount if your fear or the situation seems overwhelming. In fact, there are even times to dismount and leave the horse to his own devices. For example, if a sudden hailstorm comes up and the horse is too tense for you to handle and walk back to the barn, either mounted or leading, dismount and remove the bridle if you can (if not, tie a knot in the reins, making them really short, and lay the reins on the neck, shut the gate to the arena or door to the indoor arena, and run for help. The horse will take care of himself.

Bear in mind that this is an operation for EXTREME cases. Ordinarily, you would not want to leave a horse unattended for any reason. They are valuable animals, and they are living beings, and we have a duty to protect them insofar as we are able at any given moment.

Recall the hailstorm example in an earlier chapter. In that case, I had already ridden and was taking the 23-year-old gelding I was leading back to his stall in the far back aisle of a very large riding academy. Halfway there, he began to be very jumpy. Despite being a Thoroughbred and having raced in his youth, he was ordinarily a kind, calm old boy even when I had him cranked up to jump courses. So I was at a loss. He was seriously jogging me down that aisle, although I was shanking him pretty hard with the reins. (Shanking means to give a good hard tug to the lead rope attached to a halter, or a lesser sharp tug to the reins on a bridle so the bit won't totally demolish the mouth.) I was talking to him calmly, stroking his mane when I could and generally thinking quiet thoughts. But still, he was a mess. I got him around the corner to his aisle and as I was using my free hand to open his stall door, he whirled and kicked the aisle wall hard with his hind feet.

Yipes! I literally tossed him into his stall and slammed the door. He quieted almost immediately, enough that I could run in and dared to quickly loosen the throatlatch on his bridle—I admit that I left the noseband attached— and slip it off his head and get out.

Within a minute, huge hailstones began hitting the metal roof, and I knew he had heard it coming miles away when I hadn't, and it had frightened him and he wanted the security of his stall. He stayed calm while it passed, despite the terrific din. He was safe in his stall, as he knew he would be and had tried very hard to get there very fast.

Had I been on him when he began acting that way, I'd have dismounted. Had I been alone and unable to control him in the arena without danger to myself and no one to help, I'd have hopped off, pulled the bridle off just as I did in his stall, and shut the door to the arena, or, if I had been in the outside arena, the gates. He might have jumped out and made a beeline for his stall, but I would not have been in danger, and neither would he, really.

As it was, I left the saddle on him until after the storm had passed. Then I got him out of his stall, removed his saddle, groomed him, gave him his favorite oats and honey granola bar, and life went back to normal.

Another 'when in doubt' maneuver is grabbing mane. This is one for the more benign sort of difficulties, such as loosing your balance a little, or if the horse breaks into a trot because you ask him too hard to walk (and as you practice, your legs get stronger and you may unwittingly do that.) Just reach up, keeping the reins, and grab a hunk of mane in front of the saddle. The horse won't mind, and you'll be much happier solidly in your seat than wobbling around and miserable.

And we did talk about the halt, right? If you are seriously upset for any reason, even if your instructor is yelling at you to go on, halt. Just halt. If your instructor is too insensitive to deal with real concerns—even what to him or her might seem imaginary ones—then halt and consider, in fact, finding a different instructor who will deal with the realities that everyone's path to riding competence is different and worthy of respect and consideration. A simple halt might cut the instructor sheep from the goats, to your good fortune in the long run!

Ask, ask, ask, ask, ask

Most riding instructors are so far from their beginnings that they no longer realize that there was a time they did not know what they know now. They cannot recall what you are going through; they don't always know what needs to be specifically explained, and maybe more than once. Maybe more than a hundred times. So ask. If you don't understand something, ask. If you want to know more abut something, ask. If you want to know the reason for something, ask. And if the instructor is not willing to take the time or interest to tell you what you want to know, see the sheep and goats comment, above.

Chapter Eleven: About the Art of Riding

If you've come this far, and you're still game, there are lots of things to think about that will improve your riding and your horsemanship almost as much as riding itself. Humans have had thousands of years to develop ideas about horses and horsemanship, some of them perennially useful, some a mere fad that comes (and luckily for the horse) goes. Collected below are some ideas about horses and horsemanship that have served well for a long time, and are well worthy of being considered.

Riding theory and philosophy

Xenophon, a 4th Century B.C. Greek soldier/philosopher, claimed that riding "makes the body healthy, improves the sight and hearing, and keeps men from growing old."

Winston Churchill, the leonine Prime Minister of Great Britain during World War II, took all that to a psychological level. Said he, "There is something about the outside of a horse that is good for the inside of a man." He also admonished wealthy men not to give their sons money, but horses. Money would make a lazy fool of a boy, while horses would demand the boy's attention and engagement.

And then there was comedian Joe E. Louis. He said, "You can lead a horse to water, but if you can teach him to roll over and float on his back, then you got something."

These three quotations could almost be a 'which one doesn't fit' exercise. But the fact is, they all say the same thing: The horse, exactly as it is now and has always been, is a fundamental asset to mankind.

Riding is exercise, as Xenophon said, and, moreover, it is exercise that demands much of the muscles, the eyes—everything. And so, it keeps everything tuned up.

Churchill made the point that getting away for a ride is good for the mind and spirit, a mini-respite from whatever else is going on in one's life. And it might also be construed to mean that, in view of the horse's great strength and speed, man may properly be humbled at the same time as he is exalted for being allowed among all creatures to sit upon the horse.

Finally, a horse is a horse, as Joe E. Lewis pointed out through humor. It will always be a horse and can be taught only minimal 'tricks,' both because of its nature and its conformation. In short, it will always be for mankind a reminder that while we may be the most intelligent of the biological creatures on earth, there are still some things we cannot do. One of those is teaching a horse to float on his back. It is physically impossible, and only a fool would try.

Basic riding theory and philosophy, developed in all the years since the time of Xenophon, takes the nature of the horse into account. We realize we must work with exactly what is in front of us to get the desired result. It is as hopeless to ask a horse to be other than he is as it is to marry someone we intend to change. Indeed, in either sort of relationship, the only thing you could get out of the attempt would be failure and hard feelings on both sides. In the case of teaching a horse to float on its back, you'd get spectacular failure, and possibly an injured or dead horse from the attempt.

Anything old is new again

Classical horse training takes the nature and desires of the horse very much into account. FEI (Federation

Equestrienne Internationale, the international dressage association) judge Dede Bierbrauer of Windcrest II farm in Clarksburg, MD, it is a foolish rider who will never change plans for a horse that is having a bad day. To her, horses are living creatures like all others, and are entitled to lenient treatment when they are having a bad day.

But many so-called modern trainers treat horses like mechanical objects. If the horse doesn't behave as expected on a particular day, they simply ask harder and harder and harder. They get mad at the horse, which is about as sensible as getting mad at the rain. It is what it is. Horses do not experience malice as humans do. The horse is simply expressing who he is on that day, not with intent to annoy humans, but simply to be who he is. Maybe he's sore. Maybe he's tired. Or sick. Or bored.

So, the trick to good riding—once one has acquired a certain amount of skill so that one can truly feel the horse—is to let the horse be the horse. Influence him 95 percent of the time, but accept that five percent of the time, for reasons completely his own, he is just not quite himself and give him a break. Either let him out of work entirely that day, or change the program so that you go for a leisurely walk in a pasture rather than jump fences in the arena. Or get off him and give him a good grooming, or hand-graze him in the clover he loves but doesn't have in the eaten-down paddock he plays in every day with the other horses—some of whom he likes, and some of whom he probably can't stand.

This is a different philosophy entirely from the one you will hear espoused, still, by the majority of teacher/ trainers of riding in this country. We are a goals-oriented bunch, and we expect nothing to get in the way of our meeting our goals when WE want to.

For in this sport, your partner is, in fact, a member of another species but no less deserving of respect and consideration. You wouldn't expect your tennis doubles partner to play brilliantly the day after she lost a corporate battle at work; don't expect your horse to play brilliantly when he has had a hard day in the paddock, maybe with the introduction of a more highly ranked gelding. Or something. Something unknowable to humans, but meaningful to a horse.

Monty Roberts and John Lyon in the western riding world have done more to popularize the philosophy of equality of value between man and horse than anyone before. That's surprising to many English riders; western riding is generally regarded in this country as less 'spiritual' than English. And yet, so many English riding gurus still ascribe to the aberrant 'horse as machine' idea. Or at least, they train horses and riders as if they believed that.

Develop workable beliefs about horses

If you want to be a truly good horsewoman or horseman, you must not only learn the techniques of riding, but you must also develop an underlying philosophy, one in which the theory of riding can be understood. The techniques will work 95 percent of the time, whether you feel kindly toward the horse or not. You don't have to know theory to use the techniques and have a fair amount of success. But you will never reach the pinnacle without holding the belief that your horse is your partner, deserving of your intense consideration at all times.

That doesn't mean you let the horse make the decisions; it just means you make the decisions based on your condition, your horse's condition, his possible need for some R&R, your possible need for some R&R (we are goal-driven humans, remember), *ad infinitum.*

Treat your horses as valued friends, irreplaceable colleagues. Irish show-jumper Eddie Macken treats his jumpers to Guinness stout. They like it, and it does, in fact, have minerals that probably helps the horses out a tad.

Aaron Vale, one of only two American show jumpers ever to ride the top five horses in competition, treats all his horses as individuals, and he doesn't overwork them. Early in his career, before he won large purses in Grand Prix jumping competition, he often took on mainly 'problem' or semi-retired or once-injured horses other jumpers didn't want. He made them new again—and winners!—by riding well, and by treating each horse as it needed to be treated, not as a machine. Vale is one of the most skillful riders on the Grand Prix circuit, because he adapts his technique, too, to suit the horse.

You need not aspire to those heights. But if it works for the giants in horsemanship, can the philosophy be so far wrong?

Theories of riding

Hunt seat has been advanced, in modern times, by two great names, Captain Vladimir Littauer and Federico Caprilli.

Littauer was a Russian officer who founded a riding academy in the U.S. in the 1930s that has influenced many recent top riders, including George Morris and Bernie Traurig. Littauer believed that fundamental to good riding were just four things: unity of horse and rider, security of the rider on his or her mount, non-abuse of the horse, and efficient use of the aids.

The natural aids are the legs, hands and seat; some would also include the eyes, and some the voice as well. Artificial aids include spurs and whips/crops/bats.

Beyond that, of course, are individual theories concerning each request we make of a horse, the way we make it and why we think it works.

A lot of what Littauer gave to the sport would have been impossible without the earlier work of Federico Caprilli.

Caprilli, an Italian cavalry officer (1868-1907) became renowned for his most unusual—for the time—method of jumping fences on horseback.

The Italian cavalry way

During the Victorian era, most people, soldiers included, jumped the way the British jumped when riding to hounds. That is, they had rather long stirrups and they sat in the saddle while the horse jumped. Because the horse uses his head and neck for balance in jumping, swinging them in a rising, peaking and then descending arc, the rider had to reach out to the end of his reins on landing. This was very uncomfortable for both horse and rider. (Amazingly, one can still see this kind of 'seat' in some hunts in the U.S., Great Britain and Ireland.)

What Caprilli did was invent the forward seat, the seat ridden over fences in competition worldwide, and the basis for all hunt seat (English) equitation training that's worth a dime these days. He shortened the stirrups and got into a crouch when the horse leaped. The rider's back paralleled the arc of the horse's neck, while the deep S-curve created through thighs, calves and ankles helped keep the rider motionless above, not on, the horse's back as he arced. No longer did the horse get tugged in the mouth when the jump was big and rider's arms short. No longer did a horse have to change his balance to accommodate the weight and ungainly position of the rider. No longer did a rider jostle and slam on the horse's back on take-off and landing, and in between.

There's every reason to believe that the invention of the forward seat helped horses live longer, healthier lives, even when the horse is used hard in competition. And it has certainly helped riders to jump higher fences at greater speeds with less risk than when they sat on the horse's back and were at the mercy of any motions, good or bad, the horse made. Indeed, perched with only two points of the body against the horse means the rider can pivot his or her entire weight and balance without disturbing the horse at all, to keep in equilibrium.

Forward seat is also the seat favored by George Morris, one of today's most influential hunter riders and trainers. Morris, a Maclay medal winner, member of the U.S. Equestrian Team, and chef d'equip to U.S. Olympic teams, as well as a highly regarded rider/trainer overall, has built on the legacy of Littauer, primarily. But he has, in recent years, come to appreciate the uses of the balanced seat, another way to ride English style.

Balanced seat is one in which the stirrups are left a hole or two longer for flatwork—walking, trotting and cantering—and raised for jumping. The theory is that the longer stirrups on the flat will give a better, deeper seat and allow better influencing of the horse's way of going, that is, the smoothness of his gaits and the way he uses his body to cover ground. Raising them for jumping allows for the seat to be comfortably away from the saddle in two-point, the jumping position Caprilli invented that allows the rider's body to follow the arc of the horse's body as the horse jumps over a fence or other obstacle.

Balanced seat is something of a hybrid between the dressage position and forward seat, looking and acting a bit more like the dressage seat on the flat, and mimicking the forward seat exactly during jumps. It is the seat favored by Sally Swift, author of *Centered Riding*, although she says, "Any good seat is a balanced seat."

Chapter Twelve: A Good Walk and a Trot

Before the invention of the automobile, people used horses to get someplace. We don't have to do that anymore. But the horse's walk should still be a 'going to market' walk. Otherwise, he will not be carrying his weight, and yours, properly. He will actually tire more easily, and break down with age sooner. When he is balancing you on his back, it is best for a horse to always 'track up,' that is, bring his hind legs forward under his long body almost to (and in dressage, into) the same spot his front legs just left. Only if he is tracking up can his muscles easily support you. So, there is a very cogent physical reason for getting a good forward walking pace.

If you are relaxed on the horse and you don't feel your hips swinging in the saddle, he's not walking forward enough. Add some leg, and/or a cluck. At first, adding leg will mean kicking. But as you get stronger and begin to develop an understanding of how much pressure to use, you will begin to be able to do it by pressing.

If your horse is particularly lazy, you may have to ask him to move on at each step for a while. To do that, glance down and when you see his inside shoulder begin its forward swing, use your inside leg. Then as his outside shoulder begins to swing, use the outside leg. It can be a tap or a press, as required to get the response you want, a more forward (which means faster and more ground-covering) walk.

Until you can feel the horse's movement, which takes a while (shorter or longer, depending on the movement and sensitivity of the horse, and the sensitivity of the rider), you will have to glance down to accomplish these things. But don't concentrate on looking down. Make it as quick as you can, and then raise your eyes to the horizon ahead of you and soften them once again.

While you are using your whole field of vision, practice seeing the shoulder without specifically looking down; that will begin to develop your feel for the horse, your sense of what's happening and what needs to happen to achieve what you want to achieve.

Again, don't work your horse to your satisfaction if it means taxing or boring him. Your enthusiasm will hold for the next time, and probably increase. And you'll avoid creating a sour horse

Finally—you guessed it—**BREATHE!**

No pain....lots of gain

Warning! In horsemanship, forget the idea of no pain, no gain. If you work your horse to that point, he'll be lame. Then you can't ride until he's not lame, or you'll have a vet bill, or both. And you might actually damage your horse.

If you work yourself until you're in pain, you will have tightened your muscles. That does two things. It upsets your horse and, if he's a school horse, may make him reluctant to move forward.

And it will put you in jeopardy. For riding, one needs strong SUPPLE muscles, not tight ones. The very worst thing you can do, the thing that will set your progress back very quickly indeed, is to go running for four hours, thinking to strengthen your legs.

You do need strong legs to ride, but they need to be legs that will stretch, without bunched up muscles. By all means, exercise both on and off the horse. But accept that you will be safer with strong, stretchy muscles, and your horse will be happier. And, you'll become a skillful, sensitive, effective and elegant rider all the faster.

Interesting facts about the trot

Walking won't get you anywhere fast, but trotting will. In addition, it's fun, and it has a lot of interesting history.

Old horsemen have always said that if you want to work a horse down—diminish his energy level so he's not so forward or strong (that is, fast)—trot him on a longe line. But don't canter him; that, they say, will just make him stronger. It is the old horsemen's concept that trotting wears a horse out faster than any other gait.

Maybe, maybe not. Stephen Budiansky, in his book *The Nature of Horses*, says that if a horse is using himself optimally at each gait—walk, trot and canter—he will burn the same amount of energy at each gait.

That may be true. But few horses, especially under new riders, are going to be using themselves optimally. So I will stand by the old horsemen's tried and true standard: If you want to wear a horse out enough to work quietly for a beginner, longe him for 20 minutes at the trot, ten minutes to the left, ten minutes to the right.

About longeing: Longeing is putting the horse on the end of a 20- or 25-foot leash and asking him by voice, hand and longe whip to move continuously in a circle around you at one of the three gaits. There is a particular way to hook the bridle to the longe line so that it is effective and doesn't hurt the horse. But in general, longeing is a task beyond the beginner rider, especially at this point. The instructor, however, may well longe a horse for a beginner rider's use.

For most horses, the optimal trot would be about 8-9 miles per hour. (The optimal walking speed for a horse would be just over 3 miles per hour and the optimal cantering speed would be about 16 or 17 miles per hour.)

The trot is a symmetrical gait, that is, the left and right feet of each front and back pair of hooves hit the ground at even intervals and those pairs remain in contact with the ground for the same length of time.

Uses for the trot

The trot has always been used as a dignified and relatively comfortable way to use a horse to cover longer distances quickly. A horse can trot far longer without tiring than a human can run. It is a comfortable gait for the rider providing the rider has learned how to deal with it. If a rider simply sits in the saddle on a trotting horse without learning the techniques, one of two things will happen. Either the rider will, at some point, bounce right off. Or the rider's bottom and spine will be bumped to smithereens.

So, when humans began to ride a lot, they soon discovered that they had to accommodate the 'bounce' of a trotting horse in order to benefit from the clear advantage of using a horse's long, fast legs—rather than their own short, slow ones—to get someplace. So, posting was born. Posting uses the rider's legs, buttocks and abdomen to get the buttocks off the saddle when the horse's trot moves it upward, and to set the buttocks down again during the brief moment the horse has all four feet on the ground, between movements of the two pairs.

Best of all, unless you're on a really lazy horse that requires constant application of your leg muscles, it doesn't tire the rider much more than it does the horse. And, the rider can always sit the trot for a while if he or she gets tired of posting, or the rider can walk or canter; the canter will get you there faster, but you have to know you're on even ground and a few other things to use it wisely.

Equine and rider body mechanics at the trot

When a horse walks, he uses his head for balance, and the rider will experience some movement of his neck and head. When a horse canters, he uses his head and neck for balance, and the rider will feel quite a lot of movement of the head and neck, and often—depending on the character and quality of the horse's stride—the rider will feel as if he or she is being pushed forward from behind at the canter.

At the trot, the horse's head and neck remain level; if the head bobs at the trot, the horse is lame and should not be ridden until the lameness is gone, whether through barn care or veterinary care.

Some lameness is quite common in horses, as they sometimes injure themselves playing or working, as humans do. A good barn manager/instructor will know when to call the veterinarian and when to at least begin treatment with liniments and other 'home remedies.' If a beginner notices a horse's head bobbing at the trot, he or she should tell the instructor or barn manager right away. Often, the rider will be asked to trot the horse in both directions, or even work it at a different gait for a little bit, to see if the horse works out the problem, which can also be temporary, as a little stiffness would be for a human. As in humans, sometimes a little movement loosens whatever is tight and the lameness disappears.

The trot itself

Because the trot is a two-beat rhythm, it is relatively simple to learn; anyone can count to two in an even rhythm. At the trot, the horse's back moves up and down in concert with the percussion of his hooves on the ground. While it's simple, the sensation is unlike any other on earth. So, people must learn it. It takes, as well, some coordination on the part of the rider. Learning the two-point position and learning to post are preliminaries to learning to sit the trot and then to canter, so we will begin there.

Two-point position: Two-point is the position used to jump fences, and it is also a 'safety' position if the horse is going too fast. Why? Because only two points of the rider's body, the legs, are against the horse. As long as the rider has his heels below the stirrup iron, his eyes up, and perhaps a little mane in one hand along with the reins, it is relatively safe. When the rider is in two-point position, the extreme movement of the horse's back at a very fast speed cannot bump the rider's buttocks off the saddle and fling the rider about, potentially unseating the untried rider.

He flung himself on his horses and rode off madly in all directions.
—Stephen Butler Leacock (1869-1944), Canadian writer

How to ride in two-point

First, be sure you are stretching the backs of your legs down so that your heels drop below the stirrup irons.

Next, lift your eyes to scan the horizon.

Reach out with both hands, retaining the reins, and grab some mane with one or both about five inches in front of the withers.

Keep your back flat and your heels down.

Next, square your shoulders, tighten your abdominal muscles, tilt the top of your hips forward while lifting your buttocks out of the saddle without straightening your legs. You may have to scoot your buttocks backward just slightly to lift them without straightening your legs.

Keep your calves firmly against the saddle as you do this.

Now, you should feel exactly as if you were going to leap another player in a child's game of leapfrog. You should feel as if you could push yourself off over the back of the leapfrog player you're leaping....if you only brought your buttocks forward a bit. But don't. The position you are seeking is the one you would be in at the 'moment of perfect perch' with your hands on the other player's back in a game of leapfrog. If your torso is so stretched out, and your arms and legs so straight that you wouldn't have enough leverage to 'leapfrog,' bring your hands a bit closer to your body.

If, on the other hand, your hands are so far under your torso that a stiff breeze could topple you right over them, they are too close to the saddle; move them up the horse's mane a bit.

About you: Everyone's anatomy is different. Some of us have short torsos and long arms, or vice versa. So you may have to experiment a bit to find that perfect leapfrog position. You'll know when you've found it because, once your legs are stable—and they probably are not yet—you'll be able to take your hands off the horse's mane completely, even hold them out to your sides, without losing your two-point position.

The next trick is asking the horse to walk forward while you are in two-point. No problem. Just squeeze with your legs as you would at the seated walk, keep hold of the mane and your eyes on the horizon, and walk. Your reins are probably looping down and not useful to halt the horse. That's all right. You can either shorten them so you could halt the horse in two-point, or simply sit back down—gently—if you want him to stop.

Practice the two-point position first while halted and then while walking until you are comfortable and effective in it. You may need it when you begin to trot.

Posting the walk

Before you begin to trot, you need to learn the motion of posting. Many instructors ask new riders to post the walk.

Unless the rider is a very young child, it is does more harm than good. A very young child will think it is fun. An older child will think it looks stupid. (It does.) And an adult will quickly realize it uses more muscle than it's worth and even while being strong, the rider is probably sitting down pretty hard on the poor horse's spine. That's not so bad if the rider is a child; it is punishing to the horse if the rider is an adult.

> **Informed opinion:** If you are an older child, teenager or adult, forget posting the walk. Instead, watch some videos of people posting, or watch real people posting, before you begin learning it yourself.

So, if you are using these lessons with a young child, you can have the child post the walk, which is nothing more, for a little one, than grabbing some mane very close to the pommel, or a balance strap if one is attached to the front of the pommel on the child's saddle, and rising up and down, up and down, in some sort of rhythm with the horse's motion.

Beginning to trot: What it feels like

It feels, to most people, pretty bumpy the first time they ride the trot. It feels less bumpy to those who dance, and are used to following a partner. Those people will almost automatically move their bodies in time with the horse, and find it relatively easy to figure out the trot cadence, and avoid being slammed by the saddle.

To some new riders, it also feels very fast. It isn't, though. But it is usually loftier than the walk, with the horse's back also rising just a little overall as he pushes the hind legs and hindquarters forward.

> **Informed Opinion:** It would be best to begin to trot with an instructor present, and better still if the instructor was a careful and methodical one, like Claire Cash, owner of Afterglow Stables in Nassau, Bahamas, and former president of the Bahamas National Hunter Jumper Association. Claire says, "I am a huge fan of having several lessons on a longe line to introduce the trot; I am in control of the horse and the student can then pay more attention to the posting aspect of the trot without balancing on the horses mouth."

How to ride the trot

There are two ways to begin to ride the trot, from a seated position and from the two-point position. Some instructors refer to this as a half-seat, but that is not accurate. A half seat is a position halfway between a seated position at any gait and the two-point position. A half seat is used for hand-galloping, a gait faster than a canter, and sometimes when riding courses over fences to move a horse up, that is, to put his take-off position for the fence closer to where it should be, or to get a more ground-covering canter.

About posting: In riding dressage and in Europe, and sometimes in hunt seat, the technique is called a rising trot. However, the best way to learn it is not to rise, but to swing your hips, so I will use the term posting, the venerable, old British term.

Posting the trot a few steps

If you have very short legs, or feel you will be unsettled by a faster gait, then by all means, ask for your first trot in two-point position.

At the walk, assume the two-point, and immediately press the horse's sides firmly with both legs at once.

That's how you ask for a walk, though. So you'll have to ask much harder, and much more sharply, than you are now asking that horse for the walk. Cluck at the same time, and say "Trot" firmly. If it doesn't work the first time, use more leg, and a louder cluck. Do not shout at the horse.

If you've tried this a few times and he still does not trot, then ask an assistant to run alongside the horse, holding onto the noseband, for a few steps until he begins to trot.

For your first trot, start it at the beginning of the long side of the arena and do not attempt to turn corners. Ride the trot either as long as you are comfortable mentally (you won't be comfortable physically yet) or to a point before the next corner where you can sit down and bring the horse back to a walk. Walk through the short side of the arena, getting back in two-point toward the corner. Walk in two-point through the corner, and again trot down the long side, coming back to the walk before the corner.

Practice just these few steps of trot for a few sessions before you attempt to turn a corner if you are working on your own. If you are studying with an instructor, then these lessons are reminders and refreshers, and things will probably be going faster for you.

But remember one other thing.

BREATHE!

Halt, again

When you are bored with this exercise, return to the walk and practice halting. Practice doing it with less and less use of your hands, and more and more use of your weight in the saddle with a little hand. Don't forget to leave your legs firmly on the horse's side, too. And remember to stop the motion of your hips and buttocks as well. And remember to look up, not down at the ground in front of you, or at your hands.

Trotting exercises in two-point

When you are ready to go back to trotting in two-point, think about these exercises:

Trot around the corner

At the walk, get into two-point. Ask the horse to trot on the arena's long side. Trot him through the corner, sitting and coming back to a walk if you feel unsettled or tense at any point.

To trot around the corner, you will have to use your inside leg, just as at the walk, and your hands, just as at the walk. So shorten your reins so that you have light contact with the horse's mouth.

Informed Opinion: Some trainers will not allow beginners any contact with the horse's mouth. Others allow new riders to tug at the reins and abuse the horse's mouth. Wisdom suggests that trainers need to be attentive 100% of the time to horse and rider and introduce light—emphasis on light—when the rider is ready, not before and not after.

It is likely a school horse will try to avoid going into corners, knowing this is new for you, and you have less weight in the saddle, less leg against his side, and that your arms are busy grabbing mane. So he may try to cut corners. Your mission is to get him to trot into those corners. And it may be your opportunity to remove one hand from the mane, your outside hand, to use a leading rein to get him into those corners. It will be harder than you think, so don't regard this as a sissy exercise.

Balance in two-point

Assume the two-point position while you are seated at the halt. Ask your horse to walk. If you are having a lot of trouble balancing at the walk...ask him to walk faster. A slow, poky horse is harder to maintain balance on that one that is walking rhythmically forward.

Concept: If the horse is doing what it is supposed to do, it is easier for you to do what you are supposed to do. So, up to the level of your skills and experience, get the horse to work up to his.

Balance through transitions

Practice getting into two-point at the halt. Sit down.

Ask your horse to walk forward while seated, and get into two-point as he walks. Keep your eyes on the horizon, but use 'soft eyes' so you know what's around you. When you get to the first long side, ask for a trot. Ride this around two corners. Come back to a walk and rest. Change directions at the walk and do the whole exercise again.

HINT: Remember to breathe. You can even breathe in harmony with your horse's trot if that helps you to remember.

A better position in two-point

You are beginning to know what two-point is, and you are probably beginning to know some pain. But actually, two-point can be very comfortable.

At the halt, get into the two-point position again. Feel how stiff you are.

Breathe deeply, all the way down into your diaphragm.

Still holding the reins and the mane, rotate your shoulders to loosen them.

Yawn. Squinch your eyes closed and open them. Smile as big as you can.

Now we will deal with what really counts:

Open your shoulders toward the back, so that you feel as if you were going to touch your shoulder blades together...almost. But keep your hands where they are.

Tighten your abdominal muscles until it takes the pressure off your lower back. Your lower back should neither be rounded nor arched. (Especially in girls and women, there is likely to be a little arch in the lower back, where your belt crosses. That's OK. But don't increase it beyond what occurs naturally.)

While holding your leg position—heels drifting down, calf against the horse—begin to feel the weight on the part of your inside thigh touching the saddle, and begin to distribute the weight and the pressure down your entire leg, from where the thigh begins to touch to where the calf begins not to touch.

Now, ask the horse to walk forward and feel the shifting of his body from side to side in your thighs and calves.

Ask for a trot, and keep your calves as still as possible, while feeling the percussion of the trot-trot-trot-trot on your inside thigh. Do this as long as you are comfortable. Stop and go back to a seated walk once around the arena when you feel your body begin to lose the position.

Start, stop and restart this exercise several times until you become aware of where your body is in space and how it feels when it properly contacts the saddle/horse during a trot.

BREATHE!

Sally Swift's book, *Centered Riding*, makes a great deal of breathing, as explained in the previous lesson. Swift may be the first equine guru who has dealt in great detail with the breath. Perhaps the need came from a society that holds its breath; perhaps in earlier times, people were not so stressed that they walked around like a deer in the headlights, hardly daring to move or breathe. Or not. Whatever the reason, proper breathing is essential on horseback.

Some people have trouble breathing because of the way the inside of their nose is constructed, or because of allergies and so on. Take care of as much of that as you reasonably can (no one is suggesting nasal surgery unless you intend to make a life's work out of riding and expect to compete at the Olympic level). But beyond that, be aware of your breathing and, when you tire (which can happen easily when your muscles are deprived of as much oxygen as they need), rest.

If you realize breathing is a problem for you, tell your instructor and ask that you be allowed to rest briefly, even if you are in a class that is continuing with whatever exercise was going on. If your instructor will not accommodate your physical requirements, find another instructor. All of us—ALL OF US—differ from the ideal rider in some way. And yet all of us who want to can become skillful, happy riders with instruction, patience, dedication and compassion. That compassion has to come from us to ourselves, and it must also be demanded from instructors.

Warning! Do not take this to mean you get to 'wimp out' every time something is a little bit challenging. It just means you do not get physically, or for that matter mentally, pushed beyond the point of reasonable safety. Often, instructors are so far removed from their own learning days that they are not being mean by making demands you find difficult to fulfill; they just need to be reminded that your skills and strength and stamina and knowledge and reactions are not where theirs are. Yet.

Chapter Thirteen: More Walking, More Trotting

The best way to learn to ride is to apply the seat of the pants to the seat of the saddle. So, following are some additional exercises you can use for improving your trot, both in two-point and posting. In addition, you are ready to add the concept of diagonals, which are explained in this chapter.

More trotting

Two-point on straight lines

Begin today's work, after loosening yourself and the horse up with some of the earlier walking exercises, with a review of the best position you can manage in two-point at the trot.

To review:

At the halt, get into the two-point position again. Feel how stiff you are.

Breathe deeply, all the way down into your diaphragm.

Still holding the reins and the mane, rotate your shoulders to loosen them.

Yawn. Squinch your eyes closed and open them. Smile as big as you can.

Now:

Open your shoulders toward the back, so that you feel as if you were going to touch your shoulder blades together...almost. But keep your hands where they are.

Tighten your abdominal muscles until it takes the pressure off your lower back. Your lower back should neither be rounded nor arched. (Especially in girls and women, there is likely to be a little arch in the lower back, where your belt crosses. That's OK. But don't increase it beyond what occurs naturally.)

While holding your leg position—heels drifting down, calf against the horse—begin to feel the weight on the part of your inside thigh touching the saddle, and begin to distribute the weight and the pressure down your entire leg, from where the thigh begins to touch the saddle to where the calf begins not to touch.

Now, ask the horse to walk forward and feel the shifting of his body from side to side in your thighs and calves.

Ask for a trot, and keep your calves as still as possible, while feeling the percussion of the trot-trot-trot-trot on your inside thigh. Do this as long as you are comfortable. Stop and go back to a seated walk once around the arena when you feel your body begin to lose the position.

Start, stop and restart this exercise several times until you become aware of where your body is in space and how it feels when it properly contacts the saddle/horse during a trot.

As always, remember to

BREATHE!

Posting the trot on straight lines

Posting is the way you will ride the trot most of the time in hunt seat. Jumping can be done from a trot, and it is a lovely gait to use when you want to go out in the fields and look around and play with your horse, and on trail rides. It is the gait likely to give you the most exercise, as well, because although the horse's hindquarters will help push you forward and slightly upward as you trot, you have to flex your ankles and knees, and use your buttocks and abdomen to help set your buttocks back down without slamming into the horse's back.

By now, you've got the cadence of the trot. Each horse is slightly different, of course, so you might want to stick with the same horse the first time you go from riding the trot in two-point to posting. Then you won't have to deal with a rhythm you haven't experienced as well as a technique that is new to you.

To begin to post the trot, position your horse at the rail at the beginning of a long end facing forward.

Now take inventory of yourself.

Be sure that:

Your stirrups are a comfortable length so that you are neither reaching for them nor are they cramping your leg. Use both the anklebone check by dropping your feet out of the irons and letting them hang to determine if the bottom of the iron is in the vicinity of your ankle. But also use your comfort level.

You are holding the reins correctly, coming up from the bottom of your hand, running under the three fingers with the pinky under the reins and the thumb holding the reins against the first knuckle of your index finger.

You have 'pistol wrists' and the knuckles of your thumbs are pointing up.

Your upper arms are hanging slightly in front of your torso from squared shoulders.

Your elbows are bent so that you create a straight line from your elbow along your forearm and hand and down the reins to the horse's mouth.

Your hands are a few inches in front of the pommel and held in mid-air about an inch above the horse's neck.

Your legs are in contact with the saddle and horse every place they reasonably can be.

Your heels are relaxed downward and your toes are higher than your heel.

Your eyes are level and you are gazing softly at the horizon, while also using your peripheral vision to know your environment.

*You are **breathing***.

When you've checked all that, begin to post the trot in a slightly new way.

As long as you are in a safe arena with the gate closed and there are no riders acting wild, you will begin trotting with your eyes closed. Really. First:

Breathe. Relax.

Then, ask your horse to walk forward a few steps.

When he's walking nicely, close your eyes. Keep your legs and hands just where they are. Just close your eyes.

Then press your horse into a trot, remembering how hard that pressure had to be from your last lesson.

As he begins to move, stay relaxed and when you feel your buttocks bumped by the saddle, allow your pelvis to drag your buttocks forward and slightly upward with the motion. While the horse is lifting his other pair of feet— it's a split second—allow your seat to drop back down where it was, controlling the movement with your abdominal muscles, your thighs and your buttocks so that it is soft and even.

Do this for just a couple of steps. Then open your eyes and let your body continue the motion.

Breathe.

If you are not yet comfortable posting the trot around a corner, sit, ask the horse to walk by closing your fingers on the reins or pulling back if you need to. Walk to another long side and then begin again. You can begin again by closing your eyes, or by keeping them on the horizon.

Don't look down at your feet or hands when you ask the horse to trot. You'll have a much harder time getting him to trot if you look down. In any case, all that's down there is the ground, and with any luck, it isn't moving. (Californians might have a different experience!)

Practice making the transition to a posting trot until it seems natural to you. At first, you will be experimenting with the right amount of leg pressure, the right distance to let your hips go forward before taking them back and setting your seat back down in the saddle. That's all right. Everyone goes through that. If you're an adult, think of it as learning to drive a standard shift car with a clutch. You bump and halt down the street at first. But suddenly, it comes to you—when you least expect it—and it's very easy after that.

If you're not an adult, think of it in much the same way as finding balance on your bike the first time. In the beginning, you wobbled and couldn't figure out how to steer, balance and turn the wheels all at once. And then one day, it came to you in a flash and you never had to think about it again. This is the same.

You may get tired in a short time. It is some work for the rider, even though the horse does most of it. Don't push yourself. If you do, you are more likely to plop down on the horse rather than sit gently, and that might make him fidget or get too fast. Even if he stays perfectly equable, you will run the risk of causing pain. So quit before you're bushed, so you'll have strength and enthusiasm for it next time, and so will your horse.

Before you go on to the next practice, confirm your abilities at the trot. Be sure you are able to ride around the arena in each direction twice, at least, before you need feel you need to stop and walk.

You can progress toward this goal faster if you remember to

BREATHE.

Hints for learning the posting trot

Although riding schools and instructors call beginners up-downers because of how the posting trot has traditionally been taught, forget that term. The motion of posting is not up-down. It is a gentle, controlled thrust forth and back, with just a little lift to clear the pommel. If you think up-down and practice up-down, you will spend too much energy at it, risk injury to your horse and yourself (face it, if you set your pelvis down wrong and hard on that pommel, which you risk with up-down, it will hurt.) Think of it as rocking of the hips, back to front and back again, tilting the top of the pelvis backward as you move the lower pelvis forward and reversing that as you sit back down. Claire Cash notes that she has had some success in explaining it as a rolling forward on to the top of the thigh (femur) and then gently returning to the saddle.

If you are having trouble understanding the motion with either of these descriptions, get a tape of some experienced English riders and watch them at the trot, and shamelessly imitate!

When you feel you are ready to add finesse to your up-down trot, practice a rocking forth and back motion, whether you accomplish it with your thighs, buttocks or some portion of your anatomy that works for you. If you find you are suffering from friction when you rock forward, lift a little more with your buttocks or thighs. For many people, they have to think about that lift coming not from the back of their thighs, but from a tightening and relaxing of their buttocks. Women, particularly, often have to experiment with the most effective and comfortable muscles to use to accomplish a rhythmic, painless posting trot motion. If you have trouble with that, ask an instructor to observe what you are doing and suggest slight changes in your position that make everything more comfortable. Except for a modicum of muscle fatigue as you learn to use all these muscles in a way you've never done before, there should be no pain.

More theory and philosophy

By now, you know whether you're going to have an easy time learning to ride, or whether it will be somewhat difficult. Guess what? You're probably wrong. Virtually everyone can learn to ride, and virtually everyone has a gait that is natural to him or her. For some it is the trot, for others the canter. If you're running into frustration with the trot, work through it. When you've mastered it, the canter is coming up and that's going to be your easy gait.

If you're having an easy time with the trot, the canter may be more difficult for you, or maybe not. A few of us are just plain built to ride and all of it comes easy. But that, too, opens the proverbial can of worms. If it is all that easy, a rider may not take the time to truly learn the techniques or why they work. At some point, intuition and skill will not be enough, and the rider will need a bag of tricks to draw on, and that is the bag of tricks you are beginning to learn right now.

Here's an important one: If you are feeling unbalanced, sit down and sit deep. Your instant reaction is likely to be to reach for the neck. What happens if the horse dips his neck just then? His back will always be there, and you can sit on it, and further regain your balance by snagging some mane close to the pommel as well.

More exercises

Yoga for riding

This breathing exercise should be done at home, not on the horse. But it will give you an expanded diaphragm, and will also gently strengthen your abdominal muscles, which are useful for so much on horseback.

This is known as the Complete Breath. Begin by sitting cross-legged on the floor, with your hands on your knees, spine straight, eyes straight ahead.

Start to exhale slowly through the nose, at the same time contracting the abdomen as far as possible to push the air out.

Then begin a slow, quiet inhalation through the nose, simultaneously distending, or pushing out, the abdominal area using the abdominal muscles. Begin to contract the abdomen and expand the chest as far as possible—all this while slowly inhaling.

Still inhaling (slowly, slowly), raise the shoulders as high as possible. Now, hold all that breath for a count of five.

Slowly and quietly exhale deeply, relaxing your shoulders and chest. When you' have finished exhaling, repeat. How many times? I always liked five. But I do it every morning when I want to improve my riding skills; I admit to getting lazy about it when I'm just coasting on my riding skills. And make no mistake, this is a sport so one has to keep up one's training all the time to ride well.

Singing

This is something you can do on horseback, and it will do two things; help you relax, and help you 'dance' with your horse, that is, match his rhythms, or, alternatively, control them.

At first, choose a song that seems to have the same beat as your horse is moving in, and sing it, either aloud or to yourself. You should feel yourself relax; it's impossible to sing without breathing.

You can also use it when your horse is going faster than you'd like. Sing a song with a slower beat; your body will match it, and nine times out of ten, your horse's body will begin to move in sync with yours. (You can also slow horses down by slowing down your posting without singing; singing makes it more fun, and a good experiment to see how well trained and cooperative your horse really is.)

Getting Good At Trotting

Before one walks, one crawls. In riding, before one canters, one trots very well. A slower, more regular gait, the trot helps riders to begin to know their own balance and how to achieve it on a moving object with a mind of its own, without the added challenge of great speed and irregular motion. Trotting while posting or in two-point really well should be the preamble to sitting the trot, cantering and, finally, jumping. Sitting the trot, cantering, and beginning jumps are properly intermediate skills. However, this book will take you through enough sitting trot to begin the canter. Improving the sitting trot and canter are covered in the Muffin Dog Press Intermediate Rider's Companion.

Advanced trotting for beginners

Beginning with a review of your technique so far, it is time to begin to emphasize the mind as a riding aid.

Practice mounting.
Practice asking your horse to walk.
Practice asking him to halt.
Practice riding through corners at the walk.
Practice changing direction at the walk.
Practice two-point position at the walk.
Practice picking up a trot in two-point.
Practice picking up a trot from a seated walk.
Practice slowing your horse from trot to walk and walk to halt, and then going back up to trot again.
Practice trotting corners while posting.

Do all these in both directions to keep your horse's muscles balanced and evenly developed...not to mention your own, of course.

Review Posting

Review especially the transitions from walking to trotting on straight lines several times.

When you are happy with your progress, begin to post around corners. At this point, your main aim is to simply get around them. Don't bother yet with trying to influence the horse with your inside leg. If he bulges too far out of the corner, so that you'll bump into a jump or other object, you may have to use some significant outside rein, though.

Give yourself at least one session for this activity.

Make your own lessons

Now it is time to turn your solo rides into lessons aimed at improving the skills you will need to demonstrate to your instructor or in the show ring. (Whether or not you decided to show, practicing to the level needed for showing is good discipline for gaining deeper knowledge and skills.)

Each lesson you take or give yourself is a class; when you begin to show, each competition in the arena is called a class. Classes that measure similar rider skills and horse quality are grouped into divisions.

For the moment, you will teach yourself to ride a Beginner Flat Class, which is to say, no jumping. This class will evaluate your mounting technique, walk, two-point position, halt and posting trot. Run through the exercise in the order it is given, doing the best you can with each phase and simply correcting yourself and going on if you make a mistake.

Beginner Flat Class

Mount your horse, and enter the arena. If you are used to mounting in the arena, try to arrange to mount near the gate instead, unless there is no one available to open and close the gate for you. When you are mounted, check your position and breathe.

Walk your horse to the left along the rail on the nearest outside rail. Go once around the arena at the walk. Work for a forward walk. Work hard. At this point, it doesn't matter if your horse breaks into a trot because you know how to trot. Simply sit him back gently to the walk, using as little hand as possible, and continue. When you are halfway down the long side on which you began, halt. Make sure you sit deep, stop the motion of your hips and following arms, and keep your eyes up. Maintain the halt for a count of five.

Walk forward. When you get halfway around the arena again, get into two-point while walking. Be sure to keep your eyes up and grab some mane. Check for heels down and bend in your ankles, knees and hips. Continue walking in two-point to the middle of the next short side of the arena. Sit back down.

Keep walking to the middle of the next long side, then get into two-point and ask your horse to trot. Trot once around the arena in two-point. You may have to move your right hand off the mane to help guide the horse around the corners. Keep your eyes up. Do this by feel. If you have trouble holding the two-point that long, come back to a walk and sit and begin again when you can.

When you come back to the place where you began trotting in two-point, sit and walk once around to that same point again. As you get there, breathe in and out deeply, let your hands drift an inch or so forward, and ask your horse to trot. Post the trot once around. If you find you are losing your balance and cannot get it back by sitting deep, walk and begin again. If you are too tired before a complete circuit, walk and begin again when you can. Remember, "No pain, no gain" is not operative in learning to ride.

Rest by walking your horse. You may let him walk on a loose rein so he can really stretch his head and neck, which is a nice thing to do for him after a period of work. But keep both reins in your hands so you can get them back if you need them.

When you are ready to resume, gather up your reins, place your horse as you did before, and walk forward. Pick a spot and make a change of direction at the walk, remembering to look over your shoulder and letting your hips follow your gaze to help your horse around the turn. Keep your gaze on the horizon, not on your hands or the ground.

When you have traveled to the middle of the next side or end of the arena, get in two-point at the walk and ask your horse to trot. Trot once around the arena in two-point. Sit and come back to a walk. Walk halfway around the arena and halt. Walk on, again halfway around the arena, and ask for a trot. Post the trot once around the arena. Then walk and halt.

That was a lot of riding, and used everything you know to date. If you didn't do it perfectly the first time, don't worry. Few people do. But recall which parts gave you the most trouble, and work on those twice as much as you work on the rest of your riding.

Heading for home...at the canter

Cantering is what most people want to do on a horse. They have seen cowboys galloping across the West, the cavalry galloping into movie battles with flags waving, and people in red coats jumping over rock walls in movies about the sporting life in the British Isles.

> **A canter is the cure for every evil**.
> —Benjamin Disraeli (1804–1881, British statesman)

The canter is a great gait, but then they all are. The problem with the canter is that it is a three-beat gait, and those beats aren't even. Why? Because the horse has one foot, then two feet, then one foot on the ground at once.

The result of this unequal cadence is a rocking motion. To ride it, the rider must be both tight on the sides of the horse and in the saddle, and supple so that his or her hips can follow the horse's rocking back while the legs stay glued to the sides. The arms must also follow the horse's head, which is acting sort of like cresting waves, coming up and swinging down in a shallow arc.

Holy cow! It can be intimidating at first, but it loses its power to frighten if you wait until you are ready to try it the first time, and if you prepare yourself by learning both the techniques and thought processes that make cantering easy and fun.

Prepare yourself to sit the trot

When you have properly warmed up your horse by walking him for five minutes or longer depending on his age, ask him for a trot from a seated position, as if you were going to post. Don't ask hard for the trot; ask as gently as you can, and let it be a slow trot. Resist his forward motion with your hands a little if he sets off smartly. A horse must be trotting slowly for beginners to sit the trot; later, or if you go on to study dressage, you can learn to sit a big, forward trot.

Because you have practiced going directly into posting as the horse sets off on his trot, you'll be tempted to do that now. But don't. Instead, let your belly go like jelly, loosen the 'hug' of your legs on the saddle and horse just a tad, and grab a little mane in one hand. Keep looking up and ride four or five steps at the most. Then come back to the walk. Do this five or six times in any session. And remember to do it in both directions.

As you repeat this exercise sit for short intervals only, so that your body won't get tense. When you think you are ready to try a trip half way around the arena, begin as above, but reach your neck back as if to press it into your collar, and slump just slightly down your spine into your buttocks.

For quite a while, your hands will bounce if you let go of the mane, and that will stop or slow the horse. So keep using mane, or let the reins out.

Remember, it is better to practice a technique correctly for a short time than to allow your technique to become sloppy and then practice that for a longer time. So, if you begin to bounce at any time, bring your horse back to a walk, regroup, and begin again.

Practice the walk/sitting trot transitions until you understand how much leg pressure is required to keep your horse moving forward without trotting too fast or, alternatively, slowing to a walk. When you can do all that and also sit the trot complete around the arena three times, add an another exercise, one that helps you adjust the horse's gait at the trot, and helps you to become much more familiar with exactly how much leg and hand it takes to get your horse where you want him.

Sitting Trot Practice

Simply, when you can sit the trot at will, begin to practice first walking, then sitting the trot, then moving up to a posting trot, and back down through sitting to walk. You can also vary the sequence: walk to posting trot to sitting trot to posting trot to walk, and so on. The key is to make the changes of speed and gait when you want to, using all you've learned about how much or little leg pressure to use, and how much or little resistance with your hands.

Finally, when you are very comfortable with all your transitions from walk to trot to sitting trot in any combination—no bouncing, no tugging on the horse's mouth even when you let go of the reins—try the same exercises without stirrups.

About riding without stirrups: Riding without stirrups is not as difficult as it sounds, but it is demanding. Firstly, it demands that you relax. Secondly, it demands that you keep your position strong. But that's true of all riding; to be effective, you must be both relaxed and strong. In this case, you must also be attentive to your position.

Walking without stirrups

To ride the walk without stirrups, simply take your feet gently out of the irons. If you intend to ride a long time without stirrups, the leathers should be crossed under the pommel, with the leathers flattened and the stirrup tucked just under the front of the opposite saddle flap to keep them in place and out of the way. To do this, you need to reach down and pull the front leather to drag the buckle away from the stirrup bars. This will minimize the bulk under your leg, and also make it possible to cross the stirrups without hurting either horse or tack.

However, as you begin riding without stirrups, go just a few steps at first, simply pointing your toes outward a little to avoid the stirrup irons. Keep your leg position as close to normal as possible, with toes pointed up and calf muscle stretched down and against the horse. Allow your hips to drop just slightly so that you are able to feel the horse's movement under your hipbones. Remember to breathe, and let your stomach muscles absorb the movement, too.

Halt after no more than half the arena to b sure you are still relaxed and breathing. Repeat until it is second nature to walk without stirrups.

Just one more thing...

Perhaps there is just one more thing that will help get you ready to canter. Place a pole on the ground where it will be easy for you to trot over it. Sometime during your exercises for the day, get into two-point and trot over it.

Place the pole about halfway down the long side but not near a jump the horse might think you want him to jump. When you turn the corner coming toward it, in two-point, look at it and plan your path to it (your approach, in horsey terms). Now use your body to set the horse on that path and look up at the horizon. Be sure to grab some mane for this exercise.

When the horse goes over the pole, he will very likely change his gait just a little, since you don't know how to stop him doing that yet. Don't do anything different. Just hold your two-point and continue holding the mane...and keep your eyes on the horizon. When he has cleared the pole, go to the posting trot and continue around the arena, and repeat.

Again, do this several times, but not to the point of pain. Make sure you do it in both directions.

This exercise will get your body used to the horse taking steps that are not perfectly even, in preparation for a very exciting thing: Riding the canter!

Chapter Fourteen: Cantering

For many riders, the canter is what it's all about. At the canter, a horse will cover ground at about 17 miles per hour, pretty fast when you're on top of the 'machine' and getting a 180-degree view of the countryside. Pretty exciting! However, it can also be pretty scary.

Before you canter for the first time, go through a checklist. Check:

That your girth is tight.

That your stirrups are the proper, comfortable length.

That your horse is in a good mood and ready to work, but not too ready. If it's a cold, windy day, wait until it's warmer and calmer. Horses get 'fresh' from cold windy weather, and may be a little too happy, even well trained ones, for a beginner to enjoy the canter.

That you are in an arena with a closed gate; if you work in an open field, be extra sure your horse is calm and that there are no distractions in the vicinity.

Don't spur a free horse.
—Latin proverb

Next, work for a while at walk, posting trot, and sitting trot. Work both walk and trot in two-point as well. Work on your eyes, keeping their gaze above the horizon. Work on your hands, which is to say, work on loosening your elbows so your hands can follow the horse's mouth.

Remember: Your hands belong to the horse; our elbows belong to you.

When you feel you are riding as well as you can, set your horse up to canter.

Walk him into a corner of the arena. As you enter the curve around the corner, lift your seat slightly in the saddle; not a two-point, but a lightening. Drop your legs as long as they will go; that is, stretch down into your heels. Let your reins out enough to grab some mane with both hands, but not so much that you will have no stopping power if you need it. Do all this virtually at once.

Next, look around the corner, lift your inside shoulder a bit, slide your outside leg back a bit, and press (or kick gently if need be) your heel into your horse, or kick GENTLY if need be.

The next thing you should feel is a rocking motion, perhaps quite a large one, as your horse strikes off into the canter.

BREATHE!

And relax your stomach muscles. Keep your seat light to avoid hurting your horse or getting bumped around too much before your body understands the canter.

Before your horse reaches the other end of the arena, put your weight back in the saddle, stretch up from the waist and down from the hips, and pull back gently on the reins to bring him to a trot, then down to a walk in or beyond the corner. Walk until you are settled. When you are ready, repeat the exercise.

What if your horse simply picked up a fast trot instead of cantering?

In that case, you will need to settle him and yourself, and ask again, using your outside leg harder than before, but putting a little backward pressure on the reins so he understands you don't want fast, you want different. Bear in mind, too, that as you are relatively inexperienced even now, you may be giving your horse mixed signals, so he has to decide for himself what to do. Over time, your aids will become more precise. In the meantime, it may be that you need to return to earlier exercises until your positions are confirmed enough not to confuse the horse...providing the horse has been properly trained, of course, and also is not just toying with you because he thinks he can. Horses, more than most animals, are opportunists and will get away with what they can get away with, short of risking stringent correction, and some have a sense of humor. They enjoy seeing their rider annoyed; after all, they don't have TV, movies and books to amuse themselves with. You're it, as far as equine entertainment goes. So be patient with yourself, patient with your horse...and call in a trainer for help if your re-work on yourself doesn't produce the desired results.

Before cantering through corners, you will need to confirm your position and your comfort with the gait. You might want to wait, also, until you are comfortable letting go of the mane and letting your hands follow your horse's mouth. Horses make large head and neck movements at the canter which, coupled with the rocking motion of the back, is quite a lot for a beginner rider to deal with. So take it slow.

When you do decide to ride the first corner, be sure to look into and around the corner so that your body movement will follow. Sit as deeply as you can to the canter, with relaxed stomach muscles, and allow your hips to ride the saddle into and out of the corner. Allow your hips to twist with the bend of the horse.

Draw your breath down to your feet. Above al, maintain our upper body position. Think ballet dancer, but a relaxed and competent one, not a stiffly posed one. Sit as our grandmother meant when she said, "Sit up."

At the canter, allow, don't force. Of all the gaits, the canter is the one in which you must take most care to breathe, to relax your stomach muscles, to keep your legs in contact with the horse's side, and to ALWAYS look up and ahead.

As you progress, you will move into the more advanced techniques for asking for a canter. When you are comfortable with riding the canter around a corner, then you can begin refining your request to your horse, and your skill at the gait.

First, when you are able to allow the horse to take your hands with his head when he strikes off, begin asking for the canter by:

Sitting deep rather than rising into a half seat, and applying outside leg (or heel, if need be) behind the girth.

Rather than keeping hold of the mane, position your hands comfortably above the mane, and, as you ask with your leg, also lift your inside hand just slightly. The theory is that, by asking the horse's outside hind leg to move forward with your leg, you also ask him to lift off his inside front leg by raising your hand against his mouth, allowing him to flow into the gait.

Until 20 years ago, riders generally pulled the horse's head slightly to the outside, while applying the same leg aid, on the theory that doing so would pull him away from his inside front leg, releasing it to reach out and strike off into the canter. On some horses, even now, either method will work. On a well-trained beginner school horse, using the leg somewhere in the vicinity of behind the outside girth will work, regardless of what the hands are doing unless they are actively tugging back and telling the horse not to go.

Ultimately, you will be able to ask a trained horse for a canter without doing much more than slipping your outside leg back a little and touching your horse, and possibly squeezing up ever so slightly on the inside rein. That is, providing the horse is willing and well educated. (And also providing he is not a dressage horse, many of which are taught to canter from a touch at the girth by the rider's inside leg. In that case, the theory is that the horse will lift up, away from the leg, and strike off, gaining the loftiness dressage maneuvers require at the same time.)

Conclusion

In learning to ride, there is no substitute for a good instructor and willing, well-educated horses. However, because these factors are not found equally in every locale, riders must often make do with instructors who are not as well-educated as they should be, and horses that are not as suitable for beginners as they should be.

Worse yet, beginners often do not know this is the case until they have struggled and suffered, sometimes even suffering injuries that could have been avoided. As in any sport, it is likely that participants will suffer some unavoidable injuries. This book is meant as an informational product to help riders and parents of riders assess the real danger of the sport, and the rider's real interest in participating.

In addition, it is meant as a guide to finding the best possible instruction. Finally, it attempts to provide practice modules that can enhance good instruction and help the rider to solidify skills and progress at a steady rate, learning all that's needed to become, eventually, a skilled and tactful rider, or even the classical ideal of the 'horseperson.'

Appendices: Glossary, equine studies, and useful catalogs

On the following pages, you will find a helpful glossary, a listing of colleges offering equine studies, and a list of catalogs of equine equipment and rider attire you may find useful.

Glossary

Aerobics: An exercise system meant to improve circulation and respiration. Such sports as jogging and swimming are aerobic sports. Aerobic dancing, the sort popularized by Richard Simmons, is also aerobic and is helpful for riders. In addition to improving circulation and respiration, it helps in enhancing the ability to move one part of the body separately from others.

Aids: In horsemanship, there are natural and artificial aids to communicating with the horse. The natural aids are the hands, legs and seat and I would also add to that the eyes and sometimes the voice, although the voice is to be used rarely and carefully in English equine sport. Artificial aids are spurs, whips, and crops.

Akhal-Teke: An ancient breed of horse that is resistant to warm weather. Elwyn Hartley Edwards, in his book *Horses*, suggests the breed is as much as 3,000 years old, originating in what is today Turkmenistan. While its conformation is outside the usual scope of hunter-jumpers, its gleaming golden coat makes it a popular mount, when one can be found, as does its athleticism and temperament.

American Horses Shows Association: The forerunner of today's United States Equestrian Federation. The United States Equestrian Federation (USEF) governs virtually all English sport in the United States, including dressage, driving, eventing, hunt seat equitation, and hunter-jumper and jumper competitions.

Appaloosa: A breed of horse believed to have been developed by the Nez Perce Indians of the American Northwest. In addition to its spotted coat, the horse offers endurance, stamina and an even temperament.

Appendix Quarter Horses: A cross between a registered Thoroughbred and a registered Quarter Horse that is accepted into the Quarter Horse registry. The continuing addition of Thoroughbred blood to the Quarter Horse registry has altered the characteristics of the Quarter Horse from the original type. Once very squat and short-legged, Quarter Horses today tend to be larger, with longer legs and more scope, than the horses used on the prairie by cowboys, and are thus— with their even temperaments—a popular choice for pleasure hunters and hunter jumpers.

Arabian: Edwards says the Arabian is "the most beautiful of all, at once unmistakable and unforgettable in appearance."♥ He is correct about the distinctiveness of the horse, but many would argue the part about most beautiful. For hunt seat, the horse carries its head and tail too high. The high head carriage can, in fact, be dangerous to riders over jumps. While generally regarded as sound horses, they are often too small for larger riders, and too unwilling to accommodate their speed to what the rider desires.

Barn (stable): In hunt-seat parlance, the place that contains horses' stalls is called a barn, but so is the entire establishment—riding arena, viewing room, etc. The place one goes to ride is familiarly known as "the barn." Hunt-seat riders rarely use the term stable. Even when discussing the horse's living arrangements, hunt-seat riders rarely say their horse is 'stabled,' but rather the horse is 'boarded' at a 'barn.' There are exceptions, of course, although those exceptions are more prevalent in the west where cowboys had stables full of horses, whereas in the east, farmers had barns where a few cows and a horse might live.

♥ Edwards, Elwyn Hartley. (1993) Horses. London: DK Publishing, p. 174.

bedding (types): Horses that live outside lie down on grass or sand or whatever is there. But a horse living a good part of his day or night in a stall needs something more forgiving for his large, heavy body and tender joints, as well as needing something that will absorb urine and contain feces, since he cannot get up and go relieve himself somewhere other than his sleeping spot. Bedding can be wood chips, sawdust, straw, shredded paper, and other various composites meant to do the job without harm to the horse.

Bit: The bit is a formed, usually jointed, piece of metal that is placed in a horse's mouth and held in the proper position in the mouth by the cheek pieces of the bridle. The correct position is on the bars of the mouth, a place where horses have no teeth. The bit allows the rider to exert pressure backward, upward or downward on the horse's mouth, communicating a desire for the horse to go forward in a specific way, or to stop. Because rough handling of the bit can easily damage the horse's mouth, tact and 'educated' hands are essential aims of learning to ride properly.

blue ribbon: The first place ribbon in hunter, hunter-jumper and jumper shows.

Bolt: A horse galloping suddenly away in response to some negative stimulus.

Boot pulls: Metal or wood and metal devices to help get close-fitting tall boots onto the foot and leg of the rider.

Breastplate: A leather (or sometimes webbing and elastic) strap that attaches to d-rings on either side of a saddle, being passed across the horse's chest, to keep the saddle from sliding backward. These are not always needed, but rather their use depends on the conformation and way of going of the horse.

Breeches: Close-fitting, stretchable pants that tuck into tall boots.

Bridle: An arrangement of leather straps and buckles meant to hold the bit in the horse's mouth and provide an anchor for the reins, through which the rider communicates with the horse's mouth.

British Horse Society: Founded in Britain in 1947, this organization has a broader mandate than the United States Equestrian Federation. In addition to promoting education of riders and training of horses, it also aims to educate the public regarding equine matters, promote equine recreation more widely, prevent cruelty and neglect of horses, and secure rights of way and access for riders and lands and public roads.

Canter: This is a ground-covering three-beat gait, often as fast as 23 miles per hour. The gallop is not simply a faster canter. Rather, it is a four-beat gait, during which, for a split-second, all four hooves leave the ground at once, launching the horse forward through the air. Horses can reach 30 mph at this gait. It is used only sporadically in hunt seat, and is always ridden not fully seated as the canter usually is, but in a half-seat or two-point position. Please see half-seat and two-point position for descriptions of these two distinct seats.

Cantle: The raised, back part of the close-contact (hunt seat) saddle.

Certified Horsemanship Association: The mission statement of this group reads: "To promote excellence in safety and education for the benefit of the entire horse industry. This is accomplished by certifying instructors, accrediting equine facilities and publishing educational resources." ♥ This is a very limited mandate, far short of either the British Horse Society (BHS) or the United States Equestrian Federation (USEF) mandates. The group does not have

---

♥ Found on their website, at http://www.cha-ahse.org/mission.htm.

either the prestige of the BHS or the power and reach of the USEF, and it thus can be considered a minor player in equine sport.

Chaps: Leather garment that is worn over jeans or pants to protect the legs from brush in the field and from rubbing on the saddle or saddle fittings. While fringed chaps are usually considered western wear, fringe has become more popular in hunt (English) seat in recent years, at least for schooling (lessons) and hacking (riding for pleasure). While some hunts allow them to be ridden on a hunt in the field, the chaps worn would be fringeless and much more formal and plain.

Charge: The act of a horse coming into a human's space at speed.

Cheek pieces: Parts of a bridle that connect to the brow band and hold the bit in place.

Chestnut: The reddish coat color of a horse; also, small, horny protuberances on the inside of the knee.

Clydesdales: A draft horse that originated in Scotland. Often crossed with Thoroughbreds to make hunters.

Coggins: The name for a test to determine whether a horse is carrying Equine Infectious Anemia.

Colic: A dangerous intestinal condition that must be attended to by a veterinarian immediately. The horse first exhibits pain by pawing at his stomach. Later, his heart rate will increase, as pain and fear get worse. Preventing a horse from rolling in his pain by hand walking him until the vet arrives is important to prevent a torsion of the bowel, which can be cured only by expensive surgery and a long recovery period. Simple colics caught early are usually relieved by 'tubing' the horse, that is, administering fluids that help the horse move his bowels.

Come off: Hunt seat riders will almost never say they were 'thrown' by a horse. That would imply that the horse acted willfully in dislodging them, and hunt seat riders believe that most partings from their horse are at least partially their own responsibility. Therefore, when a rider leaves her horse's back suddenly, they refer to having come off their mount. Occasionally, the term tossed is used, but virtually never thrown.

Conformation: The arrangement of the horse's limbs, torso and head, with the legs and muscles front and rear used to move the legs the most important consideration. Conformation is judged in relation to the work a horse is intended to do.

Connemara: Not a pony, but a small, sure-footed, sturdy horse from the west of Ireland. Ireland's only indigenous breed, when crossed with Thoroughbreds, Connemaras produce very sturdy, sensible animals for hunt seat competition.

Contour pad: A fleece pad made in the same shape as the saddle.

crown piece: The part of the bridle that crosses the horse's *poll*, the ridge of the skull right behind the ears.

Correct lead: This refers to a horse's canter. The horse should reach out first and farthest with his inside foreleg.

Crupper: A strap that attaches to d-rings at the back of the saddle and runs under a pony's tail to help keep a saddle from sliding forward toward the pony's neck.

Currycomb: Not a comb, per se, but a hard rubber implement for rubbing dirt up from a horse's coat.

Dress boots: Tall boots without lacing over the instep.

Equine Infectious Anemia: Also known as swamp fever, it is a debilitating disease for most horses, although a few can harbor the disease with relatively little distress. Nonetheless, horsemen and veterinarians have been so determined to eradicate the disease, that most horses that exhibit exposure to, determined via the Coggins test, it are put down. Some modern horsemen believe this is unnecessary; for the disease to spread, a large horse fly must bite an infected horse, and then bite an un-infected horse within about fifteen minutes, as the organism lives no longer than that in the horse fly's system.

Farrier: Person who trims horse's hooves and applies shoes. Modern farriers are much more than the old blacksmith; they have studied equine anatomy, particularly the legs and feet, and equine locomotion and can often correct problems a horse may experience due to anomalies in its conformation or musculature.

FEI: Founded in 1921, the organization is the sole organization recognized by the International Olympic Committee in a total of eight equestrian disciplines, including the English disciplines of jumping, dressage and eventing. Truly international, in 2008, its president was H.R.H. Princess Haya Bint al Hussein of Jordan.

Field boots: Tall boots with a gusset and laces over the instep, making them somewhat easier to put on than dress boots.

Fly spray: Increasingly, these are natural compounds used to keep flies away from horses. Flies are attracted to horse sweat, and often plague horses in damp environments. Most fly sprays seem to do nothing, however, to diminish the possibility that a horse fly will bite a horse; horse flies have been known to walk into a horse bar and order a tall glass of spray, hold the ice. However, making horse (and the attached rider) comfortable is an important reason to spray. And horse flies, being enormous, are also slow and can often be smashed wit the rider's hand.

Forge: The act of a horse's hind foot coming so far forward under his body that it strikes the bulb of the heel of his front foot.

Frog: A triangular piece of soft, cushiony tissue that begins at the bulb of the horse's foot in the rear and proceeds about two-thirds of the way to the toe.

Galvayne's Groove: Used to approximate age in older horses, the vertical groove appears on the upper corner incisor when the horse is about ten, and reaches halfway down the tooth by age 15, after which it begins to fade, until, by age 30, it is completely gone.

Girth: The wide strap that holds the saddle on the horse. Usually leather, they are also made of various synthetic materials, as well as heavy yarn. They have two buckles at each end, and carriers to tuck extra billet into.

Grays: Horses whose coat appears in any color from steel gray (almost blue at times) to almost white. True gray horses are born with black skin and a mixture of black and white hairs, with more white appearing as the horse ages.

Green horse: Not a color, but a state of being. An untrained horse.

Green rider: Although a rider may turn green after a particularly harrowing ride, in fact, it means the same thing as green horse: untrained.

Hack: A ride with no particular purpose except for exercise for horse and rider.

Haflingers: A small, sturdy Austrian horse with chestnut or palomino coloring. Extremely long-lived, they may be active and healthy at 40 years of age; they are not started in training until at least age 4.

Half-seat: Used primarily in the hand-gallop and on approaches to fences, a true half-seat is not a true two-point, but rather is simply a lifting of the seat bones out of the saddle, while leaving the pelvis engaged. It can also be used for riding downhill or collecting a horse's stride, a more advanced technique than this book covers. Indeed, half-seat will not come into play until a rider reaches intermediate level, and then only sporadically. In two-point position, the seat bones and pelvis are lifted out of the saddle, and the only point of contact the rider has with the horse are the insides of his or her legs.

Hand: Four inches, the age-old method for measuring a horse. Today, it is done with a 'stick,' a pole and sliding crossbar showing hands and inches. A 16-hand horse is 5 feet tall at the withers, where the measurement is taken.

Hanoverian: One of the most popular breeds for show-jumping and dressage, its breeding began in 1753. Today, it is regarded as having very correct movement, exceptional strength, and a very even temperament.

Hard brush: A brush with stiff bristles used right after the currycomb to further loosen dirt on the horse's skin.

Hard puller: A horse that pushes a good deal of the weight of his head and neck against the rider's hands while also moving forward and resisting efforts to slow him down.

Hoof pick: A metal or metal and plastic tool with a hand-grip and a point (either triangular or screwdriver-shaped, that loosens dirt in horses' hooves. The plastic and metal ones have a stiff brush attached for brushing dirt away from the inside of the hoof, or the outside.

Hoof trimming: The equine equivalent to a manicure, in which the overgrowth of hoof material is trimmed away with a hoof knife, usually by a farrier, although some owners learn to trim hooves as well. Allowing unshod horses to grow too much hoof may upset their balance and comfort; in extreme cases, it can lead to deformity of the foot and death.

hunt cap: Traditionally, a velvet domed cap with short brim and velvet ribbon in the back used for foxhunting.

Today, the term is interchangeable with helmet, but is usually used to refer to a traditionally styled black velvet or velveteen helmet, rather than plastic-looking schooling helmets.

Inside shoulder/leg: This refers to the limb nearest the center of the arena, or of the demarcated space used for riding and training.

Irish Hunter: A strong, bold horse that is a cross between an Irish draft horse and a Thoroughbred.

Jodhpurs: Pants that balloon slightly at the hips, tapering at the lower leg and ending in a cuff so that they can be worn with paddock boots. The ballooning of the upper leg allows for movement of the rider through hips and knees without undue tugging at the bottom of the pants leg.

Kinetic art: A form of art that depends for its beauty on movement.

Lead rope: A six-foot length of rope or webbing attached to a snap used for leading an unbridled horse.

Liability Release: A legal form used by lesson programs and barns where people ride their own horses or barn horses to indicate that the rider, or in the case of minors, the rider's parent or guardian, understands that riding is inherently dangerous and holds the owner of the barn/horses harmless as long as the facility is not negligent.

Lippizaners: A breed of gray horses associated with the famous Spanish Riding School, which trains them in classical court dressage. They are also useful hunters, at times, as well as dressage mounts, and they have a longer than average period of usefulness.

Local show: A show at which the judges need not be rated by the USEF. Although local hunter-jumper associations may award points for year-end awards in these series of shows, no points can be accrued under the USEF system.

Longe: A French term used for the practice of a trainer attaching a horse to a long lead and causing the horse to move in a circle around the trainer.

Manure pile: Where the road apples are stored. See *road apples*, below.

Medium brush: A relatively soft brush used for getting dust off a horse's coat.

Morgan horse: A horse developed in New England as an all-round family horse. They could pull farm implements on weekdays, the family buggy on Sundays. They could be ridden, as well. These days, they are used for pleasure mounts, but seldom for jumping at which most are not too handy. They tend to be unathletic in that way and many have long backs, making the ride over fences uncomfortable for the rider, and ultimately uncomfortable and even damaging for the horse.

Mounting: The act of getting onto a horse.

mounting block: A two-, three- or four-step very stable stool of plastic or wood used for making mounting easier. Particularly useful for short riders mounting tall horses.

Near side: The left side of the horse, from the horse's point of view. It is also the side closest to us when we do the tasks of mounting and dismounting, and it is where we begin grooming. English-trained horses are all trained in this manner, making for a consistency rarely seen in any sport.

Noseband: The leather bridle component that encircles the horse's muzzle and supposedly helps keep the bit properly positioned. However, in England even now, and especially in earlier times, a noseband was not always regarded as necessary.

Off side: The right side of the horse, from the horse's point of view. Why do we call it this? Because we begin all grooming and we mount and dismount from the horse's left side, making that one nearer to us. It would sound silly to call the far side the far side, so it became the off side.

Open Jumpers: Competitions in which horses and riders are asked to jump four-foot fences.

outside shoulder/leg: The limb closest to the perimeter of the arena or working space.

Paddock: A relatively small, completely fenced field where a horse may be placed for mild exercise or fresh air.

Paddock boots: Short boots used for riding. For junior riders, they are worn for showing horses, along with jodhpurs. For adult riders, paddock boots can be used only for schooling (lessons) and hacking and trail rides; adult riders must compete in tall boots, which is part of proper attire.

Paints: Also called Pintos, these horses are registered based on their coats, primarily, and may have registration papers indicating Quarter Horse, Thoroughbred or Paint background. There is little consistency in conformation or temperament because the 'breed' is based on color alone; often, they are not recognized as a breed, but only as a type.

Palominos: A horse of any breed that has the coat color of a new penny, according to Edwards, and white mane and tail.

Percheron: A large, heavy draft horse from France, this horse is known for its even temperament and beautiful gray or black coloring.

Pinning: Winning a ribbon in a hunter, hunter-jumper or jumper competition (show) is called pinning. There are, however, no pins. Rather, the ribbons are on a type of paper-clip arrangement so they can be easily hung on a horse's bridle (providing the horse tolerates it) during photos and so on, and hung on a ribbon rack at home or in the barn to display the horse's talent.

Pleasure-horse: Any horse that is fun to ride, easy to handle and gives the rider a great deal of happiness, whether or not the horse is also used in competition.

Pommel: The center front of the saddle.

Pony: An equine that stands between 10 and 15 hh high. (The abbreviation hh stands for hands, the unit of measurement for a horse's height at the withers. A hand is four inches.) They have short, strong backs, and are usually much more sure-footed than horses. They have strong legs, with lots of bone.

Post: The act of rising upward and forward, down and back, in a sort of rocking motion that coincides with the action of a horse's legs at the trot. Used almost interchangeably with the term rising; rising, however, is more often applied to a dressage than a hunt seat. And, in fact, it is more straight up and down than the post. Despite the gentle back and forth motion in posting, when riders first begin, their instructor may shout Up, Down in cadence with the horse; as a result, beginners are often called UpDowners.

Proper attire: Show attire. For hunter and jumpers this includes tall boots and breeches for adults, paddock boots and jodhpurs for junior riders; a formal shirt with a choker collar for females or a formal shirt with tie for males; a double- or single-vented formal jacket in wool, wool blend, or linen blend or a good-looking synthetic; gloves to match the color of the boots (brown if brown boots, black if black boots) and a velvet or velveteen hunt-cap type of helmet. For women, long hair must be put up under the helmet, usually with the help of a hairnet so that some hair can cover the ears without escaping and flying about in messy wisps. For junior riders, hair can be worn (very young riders) in two braids with attractive ribbons, or in a bun held by a net with a bow close to the back of the helmet. If a male rider has long hair, it will have to disappear completely under the helmet. For women, minimal jewelry, including no more than stud earrings, a pin to hold the choker collar in place, a watch and minimal low-profile rings are acceptable. Natural makeup is also acceptable. For both men and women, there should be a belt through the belt loops of the breeches, even if it will be covered by the hunt coat. In warm climates, judges may 'excuse proper attire' midway through a show, and belt loops without a belt looks exceedingly sloppy, especially in this traditional sport.

Qualified trainers: The CHA would tell you these are trainers who have been rated by CHA. But that rating is limited in what it encompasses. Experienced horsewomen will tell you a qualified trainer is one who knows equine sport to a level slightly beyond what he or she is willing to teach. For example, if a trainer knows how to jump 3 ½ foot fences, then probably he or she should stop teaching at 3 feet. After that, the student should be referred to a more advanced trainer. This prevents students getting in trouble because of lack of knowledge on the trainer's part. There are, of course, other qualities required. One is the ability to communicate knowledge effectively to the students without berating them. Another is a sense of humor; horses will make everyone look stupid at times, and a trainer must be able to laugh at herself or himself. Another is the ability to absolutely and without apology control the environment of a lesson. Another is compassion for both horse and rider. Another is willingness to search for solutions to problems riders might present, such as lack of rhythm interfering with learning the posting trot, or a sudden attack of fear.

Quarter Horse: Horses with cute little faces and great big butts. This horse is truly American, with more than 3 million registered in the United States. The foundation horses, used for farm and ranch work as well as sprinting to get somewhere, had short legs and massive quarters—butts to the uninitiated. Infusions of Thoroughbred genes have diminished the quarters somewhat, and produced a taller horse. But they are still the 'nice guys' of the American horse world, and are still quite versatile. They are often regarded as not scopey enough for world-class jumping; however, in 1968, a 16 hh QH won the Puissance competition, jumping a 6'10" wall at the Los Angeles Forum International Horse Show, and, in the late 1990s, a Quarter Horse won the puissance at the Washington International Horse Show, clearing more than seven feet.

Quick release knot: A knot that holds firm unless the free end of the rope is tugged, making it easy to keep a horse secure, but let him free instantly if need be.

Grand Prix: Grand Prix jumping competitions pit the top riders and horses in show jumping against each other, the clock and extremely large obstacles, with five foot heights and twelve-foot spreads not unusual.

Rated show: These are shows sanctioned by the USEF, and require judges approved by the USEF. While the classes (individual competitions) may have the same names and pre-requisites for entering as some non-rated shows, because points may be earned for USET awards and participation in shows of an even higher level, the quality of the riders and horses in rated shows tends to be greater than that in non-rated, or local, shows.

Reins: Two pieces of leather attached to the horse's bit and held by the rider's hands. Western riders have two separate pieces of leather; English tack includes a buckle for connecting the two reins into one, making it harder to drop either side and lose control. In addition, it allows for the term 'riding on the buckle,' which means the rider is on a horse so well trained to the leg aids, for example, that the horse will exhibit perfect manners and way of going if the rider has virtually no contact with the horse's mouth with the reins lax and probably lying on the horse's neck.

Road apples: Lumps of horse excrement. As horses cannot be 'potty trained' like dogs, they leave the apples where they please; in their stall, on the road or path, in the arena. Horses with a sense of humor will toss some road apples with a rider on his back going over a fence.

Road rash: The scrapes and contusions riders experience when they unintentionally part company with their horse at relatively high speed.

Rub rag: A coarse rag used to shine a horse's coat, usually before competition.

Schooling: The act of preparing a horse and rider for a show by practicing the skills needed; the act of training a horse for specific jobs.

scraped off: When a nose-to-tail pony or horse feels an unskilled rider on its back, it may dash for home and run right in the barn door before the rider can get it stopped, thereby scraping the rider off on the lintel. Alternatively, if a rider on a trail ride—seasoned or not—is not paying attention, the rider can get scraped off on a low-hanging branch.

Shire: The heaviest of the draft breeds, this English horse is also known for being gently and easily managed. Descended from the Great Horse of the Middle Ages, the stallion considered the father of the modern breed stood between 1755 and 1770 in England.

Short coupled: This means a horse's back is not overly long, that its neck and tail are not separated by a long run of spinal column. This is considered to make for a stronger jumper and a more comfortable ride, especially over fences.

Slab-sided: The barrel of the horse is rather flatter than most. Such horses fit short-legged people, or people with narrow pelvises, much better than large, round-barrelled horses.

Socks: White hair appearing on a dark horse on the lower part of the leg. A sock comes up only over the ankle; a half-stocking reaches to halfway to the knee; a stocking reaches almost all the way to the knee.

Soft brush: The final brush in grooming, except in show grooming, particularly, when a rub rag will follow it.

Spook: A sudden, violent activity of a horse in which he may twirl and leap sideways, often unseating the rider. A spook generally occurs in response to some event or object that is terrifying to a horse. Some horses remain 'spooky,' that is, prone to spooking, all their lives, although the habit can sometimes be mitigated. Others virtually never spook. Most horses will spook under some circumstances. Some horses spook 'bigger' than others. A very mild spook, really more a side step or sudden halt than a leap and twirl, is called a shy.

Spurs: Metal prongs on a base that fits around the back of the boot and is held in place by leather or webbing straps. In hunt-seat riding, they are always plain, with flat or rounded prongs. In dressage, they might include a small rowel. English spurs do not have the large, pointed rowels of western spurs, nor should the jingle, jangle, jingle.

Square pad: A pad most often used by dressage riders that extends well beyond the back edge of the saddle. Often, when schooling, riders will use large, colorful square pads just for fun, if their horse doesn't need reminding of things with a crop behind the rider's leg, with which the square pad would interfere.

Stirrup irons: Metal objects that attach to stirrup leathers. They are not for holding a rider on the horse.

They are a convenience for reminding the rider of the proper leg position; rarely, they take a good deal of the rider's weight, such as during a hand-gallop. Usually referred to simply as irons

Stirrup leathers: Long leather strips that attach to the saddle beneath the saddle flap and atop the skirt. They are held in place by bars that can open up under pressure to allow the leather to break free, so the rider can be free during an accident, for instance.

Tack: The leather essentials of English riding, including saddle and bridle, and other bits of equipment such as girths, breastplates, draw reins, cruppers, and so on.

Tack room: Place where tack is kept.

Tall boots: Formal riding boots that have no laces and gussets.

The Ballad of the Irish Horse: Wonderful National Geographic documentary about the love of the Irish people for horses.

Thoroughbred: The horse that supports the international racing industry, it is also a popular pleasure and competition horse for English disciplines. They are courageous, but often temperamental. But they do have great athletic talent and stamina. All the Thoroughbreds in the world trace their ancestry to three stallions that stood in England. These 'foundation stallions' were the Byerly Turk, the Darley Arabian and the Godolphin Barb (also called the Godolphin Arabian). These three studs stood between 1689 and 1728, producing between them four great lines of Thoroughbred horses that are still extant and to one of which all Thoroughbreds belong.

Throatlatch: The part of the bridle that reaches beneath the junction between a horse's neck and head.

Track up: The action in which a horse brings his hind legs beneath his belly while moving forward. If he reaches too far forward, it is known as forging and can harm the horse's front feet. Tracking up, however, signifies good movement and balance and signifies that the horse is paying attention t his job and is desirable.

Treats: Horses love treats. They love peppermints (peppermint, wintergreen), carrots (always break them into segments a couple inches long before offering them), and apples (never feed whole, but rather cut up, to prevent one's lodging in a horse's throat). Some horses like popcorn, and some like caramel corn (avoid the peanuts.) Horses should be rewarded for giving you a ride, any ride. If you forget to bring some treats to the barn, ask for a handful of grain. Failing that, see if there's some tasty red clover your horse can't reach in his field, and offer that. If you can come up with no tasty horse treat after the poor thing has toted your lard around for an hour, shame on you! Especially for beginning riders—and also for advanced riders who keep demanding better and better performance—the poor willing beastie deserves some consideration. He's not your slave; he's your partner. Treat him right!

Trot: A four-beat, ground-covering gait that is truly a pleasure to ride—and offers good exercise for horse and rider—once you've got the rhythm down.

Twitch: A short pole, about 18 inches, with a chain or sturdy rope at one end. The chain or rope is placed around the fleshy part of the horse's muzzle, between the nostrils, and tightened by twirling the pole. It appears inhumane, but in fact, it releases endorphins so that a horse will relax during procedures that frighten him, such as being measured, or having his temperature taken.

Two-point: A riding position used for beginning riders to learn the trot and sometimes the canter; used by riders when jumping fences; used in situations in which one does not want to be jostled off the horse's back for some reason. It is ridden by making a fulcrum, using the legs tight against the horse's sides, lifting seat and pelvis out of the saddle, and balancing the weight down into the legs and heels, and adjusting as needed between placement of the rider's shoulders and buttocks. While beginners often place their hands on the horse's neck while they are finding their balance, more advanced riders will be able to use the position with their hands entirely free to direct the horse with the reins or to use an artificial aid, such as a crop.

Warmblood: A horse of a great number of breeds whose ancestry includes both cold- and hot-blooded horses. An example of a cold blooded horse is the Shire, bred in a cold climate, England, and not mixed with horses from hot climates, Arabia for example. An example of a hot-blooded horse is the Thoroughbred; all three of its ancestors were from Arab, and therefore hot, places.

way of going: The way a horse moves.

Whoa: The voice command for a horse to halt. One never says Halt! One says Whoa, as commonly practiced, the words sounds more like the chuckle of Santa Claus, a "Ho," rather than sounding like 'woe.'

Withers: The bump at the top of a horse's shoulders where the back portion of the spinal column becomes the neck.

Colleges Offering Equine Studies

If you're serious about horsemanship, the following schools offer college-level majors in horsemanship.

Averett University
420 West Main St., Danville, VA 24541
434 791-5600
Small, about $25K per year; not academically selective.

Bethany College
Bethany, WV 26032
304 829-7000
Small, about $25K per year, not academically selective.

Bridgewater College
Small, about $25K per year, more selective; affiliated with Church of the Brethren.
402 East College Street
Bridgewater, VA 22812
540 828-8000

Centenary College
Small, about $25K per year, less selective.
400 Jefferson Street
Hackettstown, New Jersey 07840-2100
908 852-1400

Colorado State University
Extra large student body, about $25K per year, urban setting, selective.
701 S. Overland Trail
Fort Collins, CO 80523-1679
970 491-8373

Johnson and Wales University
Large, about $25K per year, urban, least selective.
8 Abbott Park Place
Providence, RI 02903-3703

Lake Erie College
Small, about $25K per year, less selective.
391 W. Washington St.
Painesville, OH 44077
440 942-3872

Midway College
Small, $20-$25K per year, less selective.
512 E. Stephens Street
Midway, KY 40347
800 755-0031

Murray State University
Large, $20-$25K per year, more selective.
113 Sparks Hall
Murray KY 42071
800 472-4MSU

National American University
Small, $10-$15K per year, selectivity unknown.
Many small campuses; use www.national.edu to find
proper contact.

North Dakota State University
Extra large student body, $15-$25K per year, selective.
1301 12th Avenue North
Fargo, ND 58105
701 231-8011

Otterbein College
Medium sized student body, $25K per year, selective.
One Otterbein College
Westerville, OH 43081
614-890-3000

Post University
Student body size unknown, about $25K per year, less
selective.
Mailing address:
    800 Country Club Road
    P.O. Box 2540
    Waterbury, Connecticut 06723-2540

Physical Address:
    Post University
    800 Country Club Road
    Waterbury, Connecticut 06723-2540
800 345-2562

Rocky Mountain College
Small, about $20-$25K per year, selective.
1511 Poly Drive Billings, Montana 59102
406 657-1000

St. Mary-of-the-Woods College
Small, about $25K per year, selective.
St. Mary-of-the-Woods, IN 4784478
512 831-5151

Truman State University
Large, about $15-$20K per year, more selective.
Kirksville, MO
660-785-4000.

University of Findlay
Medium, about $20-$25 per year, selective.
1000 North Main Street
Findlay, OH 45840
800-472-9502

University of Minnesota—Crookston
Medium, about $10-$15K per year, selective.
2900 University Ave.
Crookston, MN 56716-5001
800 UMC-MINN(862-6466)

University of New Hampshire
Extra large, about $25K per year, selective.
Durham, NH 03824
603 862-1234.

Vermont Technical College
Small, about $20-$25K per year, less selective.
PO Box 500
Randolph Center, VT 05061
800 442-8821

Virginia Intermont College
Small, about $25K per year, less selective.
1013 Moore Street
Bristol, Va. 24201
800 451-1VIC

West Texas A&M University
Large, about $15-$20K per year, selective.
West Texas A&M University
2501 4th Avenue
Canyon, Texas 79016-0001
 806 651-0000

William Woods University
Small, about $20-$25K per year, selective.
One University Avenue
Fulton, MO 65251
800 995-3159

Wilson College
Small, about $25K per year, selective.
1015 Philadelphia Ave.
Chambersburg, PA 17201
717 264-4141

Catalogs

Dover Saddlery

Visit the company online at www.doversaddlery.com.

This company has a complete line of horse tack, rider attire, and other equine necessities from fly spray to wound dressing and more. If you go online, you can request a full-color catalog that, in itself, offers an education in things equine.

The company also has retail outlets, listed below:

Delaware
Hockessin
683 Yorklyn Road
Hockessin, DE 19707
302-234-8047

Maryland
Crofton
1041 Maryland Route 3N
Gambrills, MD 21054
410-451-2174

Hunt Valley
10 Fila Way
Sparks, MD 21152
410-472-9670

Massachusetts
Wellesley
595 Washington Street, Rt. 16
Wellesley, MA 02482
781-235-1411

New Hampshire
Plaistow
16 Atkinson Depot Road, Rt. 121
Plaistow, NH 03865
603-382-4000

Texas
Dallas
7529 Campbell Road
Dallas, TX 75248
972-818-3600

Virginia
Chantilly
43717 John Mosby Hwy
Chantilly, VA 20152
703-327-4423

Charlottesville
242 Zan Road, Seminole Square
Charlottesville, VA 22901
434-964-1301

Lexington
484 Maury River Road
Lexington, VA 24450
540-462-3820

Stateline Tack

Regarded as a discount outlet, its prices are somewhat lower, in general, than Dover's. However, it carries fewer top-of-the-line items. It also offers a free catalog. It no longer has retail outlets, although, for a few years, it placed its items in PetSmart stores. Contact Stateline at www.statelinetack.com, or phone 800 228-9208.

Chick's Discount Saddlery

This company offers all the same things as Dover and Stateline, but farrier's equipment to an extent that the others, which offer the odd set of nippers, cannot match. The website and catalog also offer some additional equine education for anyone who wishes to pore over it and find out what an enormous range of equipment, potions, and so on are applicable in various equine situations. Reach Chick's at www.chicksaddlery.com or phone 800-444-2441 or 1-302-398-4630. They, too, offer a free catalog.

JeffersEquine

This is the horsey part of a company offering necessities for small domestic pets (cats and dogs) as well as livestock (cows and goats.) It is a very interesting company, and well worth a look at its online and printed catalogs; as usual, the printed catalog is free for the asking, and, like the others, makes wonderful spare time reading for the horse nut....ah, equine enthusiast.
Reach Jeffers Equine at www.jeffersequine.com or call 1-800-533-3377.

Tack in the Box

While this company offers a wide variety of rider apparel, a reasonable assortment of tack and horse equipment, horse potions, horse treats, etc., it emphasizes books and DVDs more than the other sites, as well as an enticing line of horsey stuff—pillar candles and other horse-oriented home décor items.
Reach the company at www.tackinthebox.com.

Horse Health USA

This catalog does not offer tack or riding apparel, but it does offer an amazing array of products used for horses (fly sprays, wound dressings, liniments), equipment used in horse care (buckets, barn tools of every sort) and gear for doing the hard work of a barn (muck boots, sturdy gloves). A few nights spent with this catalog could easily form another significant element of early horsemanship education.

View the catalog at www.horsehealthusa.com, or call 800-321-0235 to request a catalog. While the website is interesting, thumbing through the physical catalog a few times will be more useful to a beginner rider in determining what sorts of items are useful and available for creating a high quality of horse care.

Books Cited

Budiansky, Stephen. *The Nature of Horses*. New York: The Free
    Press, 1997.

Edwards, Elwyn Hartley. *Horses*. New York: DK Publishing, Inc.,
    1993.

McMurtry, Larry. *Lonesome Dove*. New York: Simon & Schuster,
    2000.

Swift, Sally. *Centered Riding*. New York: St.Martin's/Marek,
    1985.

About the Author

Laura Harrison McBride started riding as an adult. She spent ten years studying horsemanship with a half-dozen exceptional teachers, listed in no sort of order, including:

Mehdi Kazemi, owner/trainer at Winter's Run Farm, LLC, in Jarrettsville, MD.
Peter Krukoski, owner/trainer, Fox Hollow Riding Academy, Bristol, TN.
Lisa Brown Baker, owner/trainer of Journey's End Farm, Bristol, TN.
Frank Daigle, former international competitor in dressage and show jumping, formerly trainer at Renaissance Farm, Morristown, TN.
Dede Bierbrauer, international dressage rider/trainer and FEI judge, co-owner of Windcrest II Farm in Clarksburg, MD.
Peter Bierbrauer, international dressage and show-jumping competitor, co-owner of Windcrest II Farm in Clarksburg, MD.
Andrea Leonard Barr and **Shannon Kiser**, trainers, Riverside Farm, Bristol, TN.
Lynn Newcomb, dressage trainer, Richmond, VA.
Sue Wentzel, Director of Riding, Madeira School, McLean, VA.
Tracey Hurline, freelance dressage trainer, Hunt Valley, MD.
The late **Dr. Edwin Goodwin**, professor of Light Horse Management, University of Maryland, College Park, MD.
Virginia Intermont College, selected equine professors including Beth Ravinsky Repass and Marilyn Anderson.

McBride contends that she learned as much from a handful of amazingly ill-prepared trainers, who shall remain nameless, as from those above. The intention of this book is, in part, to save future riders from suffering at the hands of trainers who need to get out of the business.

For the past ten years, she has taught hunt seat and jumping at a number of riding academies, of many different sorts, including:

Full Moon Farm, Finksburg, MD., a medium-sized farm teaching hunt seat and eventing.
Columbia Horse Center, Columbia, MD., a large combination show-barn/riding academy serving upscale Washington, DC, communities.
Woodlawn Stables, Alexandria, VA., a large riding academy located on the site of George Washington's stables; the barn where his horse was kept is the current boarder barn.
Spring Hill Farm, Hampstead, MD., a boutique riding school specializing in hunt seat competition.
Hopkins Spring Farm, Lisbon, MD., a medium-sized riding academy.
Therapeutic & Recreational Riding Center, Glenwood, MD., a large facility accommodating both challenged riders, and unchallenged riders looking for a low-pressure introduction to riding, or recovery from riding incidents.

McBride has also taught a number of students on their own farms; trained her huge (16hh, 2 in.) Quarter Horse, Major Yeats (ret.), having shown him in his prime in Tennessee, Virginia and Maryland in both hunt-seat and dressage.

She was the equine expert for Allexperts.com; has written a well-received beginning riding course for

Suite101.com, and has contributed to *Dressage* magazine and, frequently, to *Equine Journal*. She was one of three authors of the seminal equine information bank, *Storey's Horse Lover's Encyclopedia*. For Storey's Country Wisdom series, McBride wrote *Teaching Your Horse to Overcome Fears* (based on her life with Major Yeats!) and *Trailer Training Your Horse* (based in part on her understanding of the trailer training concepts of her mentor, the late Dr. Goodwin.)

NOTES

NOTES

NOTES

NOTES

A Message from *Muffin Dog*—

Thank you for reading this book. I hope it helps you with your horsemanship goals. It was fun to work on it. I hope you will find it "loyal, trustworthy, loyal and true," just as any companion ought to be.

Happy riding!

Best wishes,

Muffin Dog

www.ingramcontent.com/pod-product-compliance
Lightning Source LLC
Chambersburg PA
CBHW051820090426
42736CB00011B/1575